The E-Learning Question and Answer Book

The E-Learning Question and Answer Book

A Survival Guide for Trainers and Business Managers

Allan J. Henderson

AMACOM

American Management Association

New York • Atlanta • Brussels • Buenos Aires • Chicago • London • Mexico City
San Francisco • Shanghai • Tokyo • Toronto • Washington, D.C.

Special discounts on bulk quantities of AMACOM books are available to corporations, professional associations, and other organizations. For details, contact Special Sales Department, AMACOM, a division of American Management Association, 1601 Broadway, New York, NY 10019.
Tel.: 212-903-8316. Fax: 212-903-8083.
Web site: www.amacombooks.org

This publication is designed to provide accurate and authoritative information in regard to the subject matter covered. It is sold with the understanding that the publisher is not engaged in rendering legal, accounting, or other professional service. If legal advice or other expert assistance is required, the services of a competent professional person should be sought.

The IBM 4-Tier Learning Model is a copyright of and a registered trademark of IBM.

Library of Congress Cataloging-in-Publication Data

Henderson, Allan J., 1951-
    The e-learning question and answer book : a survival guide for trainers and business managers / Allan Henderson.
        p. cm.
    Includes index.
    ISBN 0-8144-7169-2 (pbk.)
    1. Employees—Training of—Computer-assisted instruction. 2. Business—Computer-assisted instruction. 3. Management—Computer-assisted instruction. 4. Internet in education.

I. Title.
    HF5549.5.T7 H42 2002
    658.3'124'0285—dc21

                                                        2002006056

Printing number
10 9 8 7 6 5 4 3 2 1

Dedication

For Meg, who dances in my dreams.

Contents

Why Should You Read This Book?

You should read this book because it quickly gets you on the right path to understanding e-learning. Whether you're a novice or you think that you're already an expert, you'll profit from the understandable answers this book gives to key questions about e-learning.

My own experience is that people are sometimes reluctant to ask the basic questions, and insist on answers that make sense from their particular point of view. But this book really answers the key e-learning questions. And it arranges the material in such a way that you can quickly find the questions and answers you are really interested in.

I'm particularly pleased that Allan Henderson has taken the time from his busy schedule to write this book. We've needed a focused book like this for some time. Over the past five years, Allan has been a pioneer and thought leader for IBM in the e-learning space. Along with his ability to make complex topics understandable, Allan brings a wealth of practical e-learning experience to the table.

I hope you will find this book as engaging and informative as I did when I read it in the draft stages. There's a lot here—but I think you'll find it interesting, informative, and presented in a way that's easy to grasp.

And best of all, I think you will ultimately find that e-learning is in fact a good way to improve the knowledge and skills of your workforce, and thus improve your business.

James Sharpe
Director of E-Learning Technology
IBM Learning Services

To the Reader...

POLONIUS: "What do you read, my Lord?"
HAMLET: "Words, words, words."

—William Shakespeare's *Hamlet*

I've written this book to answer key questions that business managers and trainers ask about using e-learning in their company. It's a survival guide, as the subtitle of the book says.

How Is This Book Different?

What's different here is my focus on the "business context" of e-learning.

I'm assuming that you, the reader, are a businessperson (yes, you're in business—even if you are a trainer) who is interested in e-learning to the extent that it can improve your company's business. Otherwise, what's the point? You're accustomed to making business trade-offs, and you recognize that all business tools, even the most wondrous ones promising the most far-reaching benefits, come at some cost.

This book is your invitation to join me in thinking about e-learning as a business tool. As a seasoned businessperson, you already know that businesses don't automatically benefit from just getting one more tool. The benefits come from knowing how to apply various business tools—from knowing that you don't use a screwdriver to hammer a nail. I'd like to see you use e-learning so that you use it to "really make a difference in your business," and that you do it in a way that gets the "most bang for your buck."

I promise to give you a balanced view here. I'm not trying to sell you anything except the notion that sooner or later—and not too much later—e-learning will become important to your company.

But, there are a more than few pitfalls to watch out for. To put it bluntly , there are lots of ways of doing e-learning ineffectively. That's the last thing you need in your business.

Should You Scan for the "Good Parts"?

Of course you should scan for the good parts. I know how most people read business-oriented books—in a hurry. This book was designed so you can quickly find the information you need and quickly skip over the parts you don't.

I won't feel slighted if you don't read every word here. In fact I don't really care if you start at the beginning, or read from back to front, or just skip around looking for the good parts. But a word of caution. Just because you haven't asked a particular question doesn't mean you shouldn't be asking it. Look at all the questions listed in the table of contents, and consider those that haven't occurred to you yet.

Take what you think is useful. I know that you're a busy person and have lots of other things to attend to.

My Thanks...

I can't count the number of people who influenced my thinking about e-learning. I'm grateful to all of them. I'm particularly grateful to all my IBM colleagues in the IBM Learning Services Division who provide a stimulating thought environment that is at the same time tempered with the need for practical business results. I appreciate the support of Don Ross and James Sharpe, my immediate managers at IBM, while I wrote this book. They are e-learning thought leaders in their own right and I hope they each find the time to write their own book on e-learning. I appreciate getting the capsule description of the IBM Basic Blue program, which appears in a modified form in Chapter 1, from Peter Orton in IBM's Management Development Organization. John Malpass and

Melissa Uppelshotten from IBM read some of the early chapter drafts and gave me additional insights and encouragement. I am grateful to Janis Morariu, Steve Rae, Andrew Sadler, James Sharpe, and Elliott Masie, all e-learning thought leaders who were generous with their time and knowledge, the results of which are the thought-leader interviews in Chapter 5. And I owe a debt to Kay McGowan and Philippe Therias from the IBM legal department for their speed in handling the legal review. Needless to say, the views and opinions expressed in this book are my own and are not necessarily shared by the book's publisher or by IBM. Mistakes of commission, omission, and fuzzy thinking in this book are all my own, of course. (I never needed any help making mistakes.)

Allan J. Henderson
hender@us.ibm.com

CHAPTER ONE

What Is E-Learning All About?

COUNTESS: "Will your answer serve fit to all questions?"
—William Shakespeare's *All's Well That Ends Well*

Leading-edge companies are starting to use e-learning to address their training needs. Some companies are already using e-learning in a big way.

But many people believe that we're just seeing the tip of the e-learning iceberg. The expectation is that e-learning in businesses will expand rapidly over the next several years until it's as commonplace as fax machines, e-mail, and cell phones.

Questions and Answers in This Chapter

1-1. What is e-learning?

1-2. What does the Internet have to do with e-learning?

1-3. How can your company benefit from e-learning?

1-4. What does a full-scale e-learning program look like?

1-5. Is there more then one successful e-learning model?

1-6. Can your employees really learn with e-learning?

1-7. What does it mean to think of e-learning as a business tool?

1

1-8.   Is your company a good candidate for using e-learning?

1-9.   Can companies with small budgets use e-learning too?

1-10. What's wrong with traditional solutions like classroom courses and books?

1-11. Is e-learning the same as providing information at a Web site?

1-12. How does e-learning relate to other interactive capabilities on the Internet?

1-13. How does e-learning relate to knowledge management?

1-14. Is e-learning something completely new?

1-15. Where can you find more about e-learning?

1-1. What is e-learning?

❑ E-learning is learning at a distance that uses computer technology (usually the Internet).

❑ E-learning enables employees to learn at their work computers without traveling to a classroom.

❑ E-learning can be a scheduled session with an instructor and other students, or it can be an on-demand course that the employee can take for self-directed learning at a time when it's convenient.

Tell Me More

E-learning lets your employees learn at a distance, over the Internet. For example, salespersons can get real-time training on new products without traveling to class. IT specialists can remain at their work stations while they take courses they need to pass their certification exams. And new managers can get real-time training as they perform their new manager role.

E-learning enables employees to learn at any time and any place. All they need is a computer, an Internet connection, and access to the course materials that reside on the Web.

Let's look at an example of what e-learning can mean to a project manager working at a company that is using e-learning in a big way:

> First thing in the morning, even before starting the day's work, Bill starts his laptop computer and connects to the company's e-learning Web site in order to complete the next lesson of the project-management certification course. Bill is a new project manager, and he expects to take the certification exam before the end of the year. As soon as he thinks he's ready, he'll take the certification exam online as well.
>
> Later in the day, Bill will connect over the Internet to a live "product-update training" session that is held quarterly for all product salespersons and support staff in his group. The product training session is a virtual event where hundreds of employees around the world learn about the latest product updates, see a quick product demo, and interact with the product experts via "instant messaging" and "simulation" features.
>
> At the end of the day, Bill's manager will ask him to think about working on some new projects for the company's newly formed nanotechnology group. Not knowing much about nanotechnology, Bill looks up the "bite-size tutorial" about nanotechnology on the company's intranet. Each "bite-size tutorial" takes about ten minutes and gives Bill some basic understanding about the key technical and business issues surrounding nanotechnology—so that he will be able to understand enough to accept the new project work he was offered.

You can see from this scenario that employees at their work computer can:

1. Take training courses for skill certification; these courses can be taken at the employees' convenience in bite-size pieces over weeks or months. This was the project-management certification course in the example.

2. Participate in regularly scheduled "live-update" training on products, processes, or other topics that are important

to the business. This was the product-update training in the example.

3. Take on-demand, self-directed training for short topics important to your business.

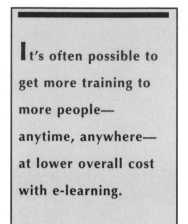

It's often possible to get more training to more people— anytime, anywhere— at lower overall cost with e-learning.

Depending on the topic being taught, e-learning can be instructor-led or self-directed (without instructor). Some e-learning is designed to be completed at scheduled times, and other kinds of e-learning are completely unscheduled: Students can take the course at their convenience.

While e-learning comes in a variety of styles and sizes, all of the e-learning varieties share the goal of getting knowledge and skills training to employees more quickly, more effectively, and often at lower cost.

1-2. What does the Internet have to do with e-learning?

❏ The Internet provides a delivery infrastructure that enables e-learning to be effective in the business world.

Tell Me More

The Internet makes all the difference. Since the Internet is changing almost everything about modern life, we shouldn't be too surprised that it's changing how people learn in the workplace. (I am using "Internet" here in the broad sense of "anything accessible from a Web browser like Netscape Navigator or Microsoft Internet Explorer". While there is certainly an important difference between the public Internet, a corporate intranet, extended extranets, and so on, in a sense, it's all the "Net.")

❏ The Internet connects almost everyone, or at least everyone in the business world. In most businesses today, the computer connected to the Internet is as a common as the telephone.

If the training course is on the Internet, you don't have to print thousands of CDs or print hundreds of copies of class materials (and have them get lost or delayed in transit) in order to get training to your employees. And the most up-to-date version of the training course can always be available when it's right there on the Web.

❑ The Internet is a virtually free distribution system. In the old days, the cost of transmitting (or "delivering") technology-based training was a significant chunk of the overall cost— you'd first have to set up your own private network, which was a complicated and costly undertaking, only attempted by the brave at heart.

But most businesses now have already connected their employees to the Internet for other reasons—so the incremental cost of using it for training can be almost nothing. (Of course, if you have instructor-led classes, the instructor is still a cost, but not the travel expenses for the instructor, who doesn't need to travel anymore.)

And we can safely expect that the Internet will continue to transform learning, just as it continues to transform business as a whole, well into the foreseeable future.

1-3. How can your company benefit from e-learning?

E-learning can help your business so that:

❑ Employees can learn without traveling to class—the training is delivered right to their computer. This means that you can save on travel costs and that employees don't have to be away from work for extended periods of time.

❑ Employees can learn at their own convenience—many e-learning courses don't have rigid start and end times. Many people can learn much better when they can learn at a convenient time.

❑ Employees can sometimes learn in ways that are more effective than what they see in the traditional company classroom. Many people can learn better when the material to be learned is in bite-size pieces, or spread over several weeks instead of packed into a couple of intensive days.

❑ Companies can get more bang for their education buck—especially when you can reduce existing expenses associated with going to class, and you structure e-learning to take advantage of its strengths.

Training magazine reports that corporations can save 50 to 70 percent of their overall training costs by replacing traditional training with e-learning.

A WR Hambrecht & Co. study says that $500 million was spent on Internet training in 1999, and is expected to reach $7 billion in 2002. And projections from there go straight through the roof.

IBM achieved $375M in benefits from its use of e-learning in 2001

More than 33 percent of IBM's own employee training is done via e-learning

Tell Me More

In the business world, learning is not an end in itself. "Learning for learning's sake" is good for an academic institution, but in the business world learning is a means to an end. That end is the improved performance of the workforce. And that improved performance should directly correlate to a more competitive company.

You should get excited about e-learning only to the extent that you can clearly see how it can improve your business. So, what's there to get excited about from a business perspective? Here are some things:

❑ *Cost savings.* Companies regularly work to drive down costs in today's increasingly competitive economy, and they find that existing education costs can be dramatically reduced with e-learning, especially as travel costs to classroom courses are eliminated.

❑ *Learning quality.* E-learning can be more flexible (learning at a convenient time, learning spread over weeks, etc) and can even provide a higher quality of learning. Many students learn much better and retain the learning much longer when permitted to learn at their own pace. And many students find that learning a little each day can be more effective than the week-long classroom approach.

❑ *Rapid training rollout.* With accelerated product cycles, you can't wait to roll out training over a matter of months. E-learning can often be delivered quickly across the organization so that all the people who need training can get it in the shortened timeframe.

❑ *Coping with shortened knowledge lifecycles.* In the old days, an employee could be expected to use skills or knowledge for decades. Today, however, knowledge and skills can go out of date in a matter of months. High-tech firms are not surprised when engineers and programmers are expected to learn fundamentally new skills every couple of years.

Most businesspeople are first attracted to e-learning by the promise of reduced costs. *Training* magazine reports that companies can save between 50 and 70 percent when they replace instructor-led training with e-learning. Most of the hard savings in the short term are in travel and living costs.

In short, e-learning can let you do these two things:

1. You can replace learning events that are already taking place in a classroom setting or at least as a face-to-face presentation. You can replace a costly series of classroom courses with a sequence of e-learning courses or events.

2. You can create new learning opportunities; you can do training that is almost impossible to do when everyone has to gather face to face. You can, for example, train a group of new managers in bite-size chunks over a year's time even if the managers are widely distributed in locations around the world.

But e-learning isn't a magic token that will automatically improve your business if you simply touch it. Like any business tool, it needs to be used with some skill and judgment. It's possible to implement e-learning poorly—and lose the promised benefits—if you're not paying close attention to how you're going about it. To do it right, the training material needs to be well crafted. The students need to be motivated to use the e-learning. And the training needs to be easily accessible.

You don't use a screwdriver to hammer a nail, even if the price of the screwdriver is a third of the cost of that of a hammer.

1-4. What does a full-scale e-learning program look like?

❑ IBM's management development training is a good example for starting to see how to apply a robust, successful e-learning program.

❑ This program trains 30,000 new managers per year worldwide.

❑ The program comprises extensive online learning modules, online learning support from designated management coaches, and learner collaboration.

❑ This extremely effective program is a blended solution; besides the online parts, it also includes a five-day classroom session to round out the learning experience.

Tell Me More

While most of us have spent years and years in a classroom setting, our experience with e-learning is often much more limited. But it's important that you have a feel for how a successful e-learning program can be structured and applied.

The rest of this answer section will look at a successful implementation of e-learning—IBM's management development training. The IBM management development training described here is not the only way to make e-learning work successfully, but it's a useful starting point. (Chapter 2 will describe other possible case studies for you to look at after you read this one.)

IBM's management development program needs to train more than 30,000 new and experienced managers in more than fifty countries each year. Traditionally, IBM managers attended regular traditional classroom training courses. But e-learning raised the question of whether that traditional approach was still the best approach. IBM's challenge, therefore, was to maintain a rich learning experience—while still ensuring that it was practical, cost-effective, and engaging to the students.

In 1999, IBM rolled out an e-learning program called "Basic Blue for Managers." The course and its underlying learning model were honored as being among the top ten employee-development models by Brandon Hall's Corporate E-Learning Benchmarking 2000 in addition to achieving three Excellence in Practice awards from the American Society for Training & Development: "Workplace Learning and Development"; "Organizational Learning"; and "Electronic Learning Technologies."

IBM's management development training is a series of learning interventions that stretches over a period of months and provides IBM managers around the world with an integrated program available 24/7, directly from their desktop or laptop computers. "Basic Blue for Managers" is a year-long process through which a new IBM first-line manager achieves mastery in the skills required to be an effective IBM leader and manager.

Basic Blue begins when a new IBM manager enrolls with twenty-three other new managers. They are directed to "The First 30 Days' QuickView," which teaches the appropriate actions to take with their new employees and their second-line managers and provides a series of online tools as well as checklists for the first month on the job. The new manager is supported throughout the year not only by the extensive material contained in the online LearningSpace media center, but also by receiving coaching from the second-line manager, via an online coaching simulator and other online coaching materials.

During the first twenty-five weeks, the new manager spends about two hours per week completing the online mastery tests in leadership and people-management skills. The new manager works through another series of self-directed modules and a dozen online human resources simulations, which teach the user how to access and search the vast HR data base in order to be able to find the information to appropriately address any HR issue or concern. The goal here is to "teach the manager how to fish." The new manager then completes an assessment tool for the manager's thinking styles, which is used in the classroom portion of the training (described next).

The five-day in-class learning lab is held midway through the year-long process at one of IBM's learning centers around the world. Here the new managers join the other new managers with whom they have been collaborating online. The five-day classroom session is devoted to establishing peer networks, developing face-to-face teaming and collaboration, and building on the management skills that began with the online learning. Students have found that they are able to jump into this more complex learning environment quickly since the basic information transfer has already occurred in the earlier online parts of the course. The classroom portion of the training can thus run at a much higher skill level than a typical management training course because it can focus on those learning situations that are truly done best in a face-to-face situation. In short, it can start where other classroom courses end.

The new managers then return to the next e-learning portion of the course. They work online in a collaborative fashion in six-person teams to learn more about leadership skills for the final twenty weeks of the program.

At the conclusion of the year-long learning process, the new manager is awarded qualification as an IBM manager.

The results of Basic Blue are impressive. More than 4,000 managers have completed the training and received it enthusiastically. Basic Blue enables managers to learn five times as much material as was previously delivered in IBM's classroom-only approach.

Once again, the "Basic Blue" approach is not the only way to create a successful e-learning program. There are many others. The next question/answer section explains further ways of applying e-learning.

1-5. Is there more than one successful e-learning model?

❑ E-learning as described in the previous question/answer section (the IBM management development training curriculum) is certainly not "the only way" to do e-learning.

❑ The e-learning approach you take will depend on understanding what learning situation you need to address from a business point of view and then adjusting e-learning to meet the needs of that situation.

Tell Me More

Yes, there are many other ways of applying e-learning besides the IBM management development training example in the previous question/answer section.

The IBM management development training example is a robust solution. It's useful to think of the IBM management development training example as a "full-course banquet." It has all the meal courses—from appetizers to dessert—and it's aimed at a large crowd of people. But you don't always need to be serving "full course banquets." Sometimes you might want:

❑ A simple meal at a restaurant for a medium-size group of your friends and relatives
❑ A home-cooked meal for your immediate family
❑ Fast food for yourself

The bottom line is that the way you apply e-learning to your business will depend completely on the "learning situation" (or situations) your business is facing. If you only have time to grab a fast-food hamburger, you're not going to step into a restaurant that serves leisurely full-course meals.

Here's a quick summary of the main areas where e-learning can be used effectively today:

Type of Training Needed	Features
Technical Training	You can teach how to use products like Microsoft Word and Excel, or how to program in C++, or how to be a Linux System Administrator. This type of training can include parts that are self-study, parts that are instructor-led, and parts where the student practices the technical skills on a simulator

Type of Training Needed	Features
	or with a virtual connection to a real system running the application or product being learned.
Professional Knowledge and Skills Training	You can teach such professional skills as negotiating, running meetings, coaching, and team dynamics to students in many locations in your company. This type of training can include parts that are self-study (for knowledge transfer) and parts that are instructor-led (for skills transfer).
New-Job-Role Training	You can teach employees how to perform a new job role. New managers, for example, generally require new knowledge and new skills. So do "new hires." This type of training can be partly self-study and partly interactive where the students work with an instructor or with other students.
"Update" Training	You can update employees who have already been trained in a topic but now need to get up to speed on the latest state-of-the-art developments. Again, this can be self-study or instructor-led.
"Tip of the Iceberg" Training	There are many situations where an employee needs to know "a little" about a topic but does not need to become an expert. For example, a technical employee can learn the basics of marketing, a project manager can learn the basics of databases, and a manager can learn the basics of corporate finance. This "tip of the iceberg" type of learning lends itself to a self-study, on-demand style—but can be successful as instructor-led also.

The key thing to realize from a business point of view is that these training scenarios are not all equal. Some will have higher stakes for your business than others. And for a specific scenario, there is often more than one way of implementing it.

Note: Chapter 2 contains a series of e-learning case studies that gets very specific about how e-learning can be used in specific situations. Look there for more about how e-learning can be applied.

1-6. Can your employees really learn with e-learning?

❑ Yes, research shows that e-learning works just as well as classroom learning.

❑ Some things can be more effective when done in a classroom environment.

❑ You can use e-learning to teach almost anything that a business needs to teach.

Tell Me More

Research studies sponsored by businesses and universities indicate that e-learning works about as well as classroom learning. (That doesn't mean that classroom learning was ever 100 percent effective, of course.) But it's good to know that education quality need not degrade as you move to e-learning.

Now it's true that, in specific cases, you'll have employees who will find it difficult to learn in an e-learning environment—just as some people have problems with virtual meetings over the phone. Usually, this is a small percentage of your employee population.

So, your expectations should be that e-learning can handle essentially the same training work as classroom learning. But while you can teach almost anything with e-learning that you can in the classroom, there are still a few constraints you'll need to use your judgment about. Some learning situations lose a lot of effectiveness without face-to-face interaction. For example:

❑ Exercises in a "learning to negotiate" course are much more effective if the instructor is in the same physical space as the student. The same goes for some of the workshop exercises of sales training. Or anything else that really demands one-on-one, face-to-face interaction.

❑ Lab exercises for some tasks need access to the real hardware. A student can learn to repair a copier or learn to change a tire more effectively if she can physically manipulate the item.

Now that doesn't mean that e-learning can never be used in these situations. It only means that you'll have to take extra care when you want to apply e-learning to them. You might be faced with a situation where you simply can't get the students into the classroom—then you'll have to decide whether you can live with the partial results that e-learning might give you.

1-7. What does it mean to think of e-learning as a business tool?

❏ What we're talking about in this book is not knowledge for the sake of knowledge. We're talking about knowledge and skills for the sake of your business.

❏ This is not the university environment, or even the secondary-school environment. This is training aimed at supporting the goals of your business.

Tell Me More

Thinking of learning as a business tool that can help improve the bottom line is a different perspective from thinking about learning in a university context or even about learning as self-improvement for an individual. This is not knowledge for the sake of knowledge. This is knowledge and skills for the sake of business. For example: It's not learning Ancient Greek or learning to play the piano. It is learning C++ because your employees need it on the job. It's learning negotiating skills because your employees need them on the job.

When thought of as a business tool, learning has to serve the needs of that business. It's critically important, then, to:

❏ Shape learning in a specific business direction.
❏ Shape learning to a specific level of proficiency.
❏ Shape learning within a specific timeframe.

In short, the measure of success is not whether the student learned something. The measure of success if whether it makes a difference to your business.

1-8. Is your company a good candidate for using e-learning?

❑ It's safe to say that, in the long term, from five to ten years, all companies are good candidates for using e-learning.

❑ In the short term, from right now to a year or so from now, you have to think about whether your company's training situations are a good fit with today's strengths of e-learning.

Tell Me More

The following table can help you determine if your company could immediately use e-learning in an effective manner.

Question	Response
1. *Do you need to train a geographically dispersed work force with employees in many different cities or countries?*	YES: You could get people from different geographic locations together for "virtual" learning experiences with e-learning.
2. *Do you have company programs or initiatives that often require many employees to learn new things in a short period of time?*	YES: You could use e-learning to get training dispersed to employees very quickly, without waiting for a face-to-face meeting.
3. *Do you expect many of your employees to regularly engage in lots of training experiences?*	YES: Many employees find it better to learn at their own convenience.

Question	Response
4. *Is your workforce connected to the Internet or to an intranet within the company?*	YES: You could start to use e-learning because the distribution infrastructure is already in place.
5. *Does your company compete for talent with other companies?*	YES: A strong e-learning program could be valuable to help you retain talented individuals.
6. *Are you looking to reduce the cost of classroom training?*	YES: You could start to look at e-learning for cost savings, especially for travel expenses.
7. *Are you are looking for more flexible and higher quality learning experiences for your employees?*	YES: You could use e-learning to provide learning approaches that are not possible in a typical classroom setting. For example: learning in bite-size pieces over a period of weeks, learning at a time that is convenient for the student, learning that has collaboration with students from all over the world.
8. *Does your company sell products/services that require your employees to constantly learn new things to keep up to speed? For example, engineers in a high-tech company will always need to be learning to keep up with the ever-progressing state of the art.*	YES: You can use e-learning to help employees keep themselves up to speed on your company's products and services. E-learning "events" could be regularly scheduled or available on demand.

Question	Response
9. *Are your company's product cycles shortening and does the project training time need to be shortened as well?*	YES: You can use e-learning to train more people in a shorter amount of time than you could roll through a series of traditional classroom courses.

1-9. Can companies with small budgets use e-learning too?

- ❏ Yes, e-learning doesn't always require a large budget.
- ❏ One approach is to "lease" or "rent" your e-learning capability instead of building it and maintaining it yourself.
- ❏ Another approach is to operate a Chevy instead of a Porsche.

Tell Me More

You might get the impression that e-learning is only for the really large corporations with really large training budgets. But there are inexpensive ways to do e-learning too.

The first thing to do if you have a small budget is to look at "renting" or "leasing" your entire e-learning solution instead of building it yourself. Or you might want to "rent" a part of your e-learning solution and build only part of it. This is just like many other business decisions you'll make—do you buy the trucks for shipping your products around the country or do you send things via Federal Express and UPS? Do you rent your office space, or do you buy the building? Do you create your own workshops for all your training needs or do you send employees to training companies and associations?

There are a number of learning vendors who have e-learning courseware available from an existing Web site. You should be able to contract one of them to deliver e-learning courses to your employees at subscription (discount) prices. The key consideration here is whether the learning vendor already has the courseware you want to use to train your employees. If you need training in Microsoft Office, and the vendor has that training, then it's a good fit. If you need training in your own company's policies and practices for new hires, then the vendor is not going to have that sitting on the shelf.

Another approach is to run a Chevy instead of a Porsche. There are lots of ways to implement e-learning, some more expensive than others. (Specifics about e-learning costs are covered later in this book.) The effectiveness of a training course is related, but not strictly related, to the amount of money you spend on it. It's not always true that you automatically get more effective training by spending even more money on it. Think of the film industry. What makes a good film is the story, and sometimes an action-oriented story can be enhanced with special effects. But there are many instances of action-oriented films spending lots of money on special effects yet having a poor story. These films usually fail at the box office. In the same way, if you have sound instructional content, you might have a variety of e-learning methods (and a range of costs) for implementing it with e-learning. Going back to the film example, you might not have all the special effects, but you'll have an effective movie.

Let's make that more specific: For little incremental cost, you can run a short correspondence course using e-mail. You can send the assignments to the students as e-mails or as file attachments to the e-mails. The students can complete each assignment and e-mail it back to the instructor for comment and feedback. This is a rudimentary use of the technology, but if the assignments are constructed in a sound manner so the student learns the material step-by-step, then this shoestring budget approach can be very effective. There are obvious drawbacks to this approach, and you wouldn't want to do everything this way, but it can work in selected instances. (In fact, I know it works because I've done it myself.)

The following table summarizes some key questions to help you scope your learning problem. But will e-learning help you solve your learning problem? It depends on a lot of factors, which you'll be better able to judge after you read Chapters 2, 3, and 8.

Question	Answer
What is your learning problem?	It might be providing "product updates" to your sales force. Or, it might be to provide a general e-learning solution for all employees taking any kind of course.
	It's very important to write down the learning problem so that everyone involved with solving it can see the same thing.
How many students are affected?	Are you training one hundred people every quarter or thousands of people every day?
	Or do you only have thirty-five people to train once a year?
How fast does the problem need to be solved?	Do you need it next month or next year?
	Do you have a deadline for getting everyone trained?
	Is this a strategic direction for you? Or is it tactical leading to strategic or just tactical?
How much time can students spend in the course?	Can students attend for only an hour a day? Or can they spend all day for a matter of weeks?
How much interactivity do the students really need?	Is an instructor necessary or just "nice to have"?
	Is interaction with other students necessary or just "nice to have"?
How fast will the material go out of date?	How will you: ❏ Update course content? ❏ Handle problems? (Will you have a help desk?)

Question	Answer
What kind of tracking and measurements are needed?	Do you need daily reports of who took what? Monthly reports? Do you need to know who passed what test?

1-10. What's wrong with traditional solutions like classroom courses and books?

- ❑ Nothing. They'll continue to work. Don't throw them away.
- ❑ Nothing was wrong with radio or movies either. While TV took over mass entertainment, radio programs and movies still exist for specific market segments.

Tell Me More

The traditional learning solution that still leaps to the mind of most companies is to gather everyone in a classroom and present the material. It might be a simple presentation-style lecture class or a full-blown class with lectures, hands-on exercises, and group projects.

Another traditional solution is to send a "how to" document (or book) to anyone who needs it.

Yet another traditional solution is to tell something to the company's managers and then require that the managers tell the employees who work for them. This might be accompanied with a package of PowerPoint charts and some questions and answers so the managers keep to the main message.

These traditional solutions have drawbacks:

- ❑ The time it takes to reach all (not just some) of the employees who need the training
- ❑ The cost of reaching all (not just some) of the employees

Earlier technologies for learning at a distance included CD-ROMs, audiotapes, and videotapes. But the Internet is poised to overtake them within a few years because of (1) accessibility and (2) familiarity.

❏ *Accessibility:* Previous technologies stored information on physical media. You had to physically ship the item (CD-ROM, tape, etc.) to the student. It could get lost in transit, or it could get left at work when the student wanted to study it at home. Or the student could spend hours at work waiting for the AV department to ship over a videotape player and TV set. And if the course material is updated frequently, the student has to be sure he has the most recent CD-ROM. The Internet, on the other hand, lets you get at the right training material from almost any computer, almost anywhere.

❏ *Familiarity:* As more and more people use the Internet for e-mail and shopping, a lot of the technological fear factor will fade away. It's already disappeared for the more technical students and for college students. While some unfamiliarity will remain, it should quickly disappear for most segments of the population.

Furthermore, most of the earlier technologies that could be widely distributed were one-way instruction. While a book on piano playing might be very complete, most people can't learn to play the piano this way. They need an instructor for encouragement and feedback and to point out when they're using the wrong fingering. Not to mention timing, volume, smoothness, and emotion!

You can think of e-learning over the Internet as being a lot like television in the 1950s. At that time, most people got their entertainment from movies, radio, books, and magazines. But television has taken over much of the mass entertainment market. Movies, radio, books, and magazines are much more niche players today. But it's important to point out that movies, radio, books, and magazines have not been wiped out completely. And in the same way, earlier technologies and methods for learning will not be wiped out by the coming of e-learning. They will all continue to exist side-by-side, with e-learning taking up more and more of the lion's share of the market.

1-11. Is e-learning the same as providing information at a Web site?

❑ It's different—just as learning to speak French is different from looking into an English-French dictionary.
❑ But if you already know how to speak French, having an online dictionary for looking up the words you've forgotten can be very handy.

Tell Me More

E-learning is different from putting together a typical Web site that holds lots of facts. Web sites have traditionally been involved in providing marketing information or technical information to users. Information can be part of a learning solution but, in most cases, NOT the whole thing. There is a lot more to doing Internet-based training than putting a lot of reference information on a Web site.

You can think of e-learning as a guided tour from a beginning skill point to a learning objective. At the end of an e-learning experience, the student will have learned specific new knowledge or a specific new skill—the student is guided step-by-step in a way that almost always meets the learning objective.

It's the difference between taking piano lessons and reading all the index entries in the encyclopedia about piano playing. You'll find the same facts in both places. But the class will focus and arrange the facts, and the instructor will guide you (with encouragement and feedback on your performance) so you can actually play after a number of lessons.

1-12. How does e-learning relate to other interactive capabilities on the Internet?

❑ E-learning always has a specific instructional objective.
❑ You might learn things as a side-effect from other interactive experiences on the Internet, but that doesn't make those experiences e-learning.

Tell Me More

One way to tell e-learning from other interactive activities on the Internet is that e-learning has a specific instructional objective. With e-learning, an instructional objective might be "At the end of this course, you will be able to speak conversational French at a beginner's level."

It's true that you can learn as a side-effect from other interactive Web activities, but that doesn't mean you should think of them as e-learning.

Here are some other interactive activities that are not e-learning even though you might learn something as a side effect of using them.

❑ *E-meetings.* This is the Web analog of the regular face-to-face meeting. It can be one person with one other person or a group of people. You might gather a lot of information in a meeting. But few meetings have the goal of getting everyone to a specific knowledge/skill level.

❑ *E-mail.* You can get a lot of informational facts by interacting with someone, especially if he's an expert, via e-mail. But few e-mails have the goal of getting you to a specific knowledge/skill level.

❑ *Instant messaging.* You can gain a lot of knowledge by interacting with someone via instant messaging. But that doesn't make it an e-learning experience; few instant messages have the goal of getting everyone to a specific knowledge/skill level.

❑ *Virtual reality experiences (like a walk through a building before it's built).* You can gain a lot of insight into the building's look and feel this way, but few such experiences have the goal of getting everyone to a specific knowledge/skill level.

Of course, all these items can also be built into more formal e-learning experiences.

Again, remember that an e-learning experience is structured to meet a specific instructional objective with the aim of getting a student to a specific knowledge level or skill level.

1-13. How does e-learning relate to knowledge management?

❑ Knowledge management is related to e-learning, but it's not the same thing.
❑ Knowledge management is aimed at keeping facts, data, and information at people's fingertips—for those people who are already skilled at doing the job.

Tell Me More

Knowledge management (KM) attempts to codify and make retrievable all of the knowledge that floats around a company—both explicit and implicit knowledge. KM is an integrated, systematic approach to identifying, managing, and sharing all of an enterprise's information assets. Such assets include databases, documents, policies, and procedures as well as previously unarticulated expertise and experience held by individual workers. You can immediately see that this is different from what might happen in a "virtual classroom."

Knowledge management is a lot more like a virtual library—not just a library of formal documents, but a library that also includes informal documents and informal discussion, stored in a fashion that allows you to retrieve what you need. (What good is a library if you can't get to just the right piece of information?) Knowledge management technologies include threaded discussion groups, chat rooms, synchronous meeting tools, and other collaborative software. What's important from a knowledge management point of view is not just what's in the formal documents or company databases; it's also what's in the "current conversation among the employees" who are working on the state of the art. More sophisticated tools, such as knowledge databases that archive unstructured knowledge resources in ways that can quickly be found through keyword searches, form the next step in integrating e-learning and knowledge management. As e-learning developers work out ways to store and manage learning content in modular, object-based formats, learning content could be served to users together with other knowledge resources from the same knowledge repository.

Pretend you're standing at the edge of a forest. You want to hike into the forest and climb to the top of the mountain beyond. If you're an experienced woodsman, you can walk directly into the forest, and there's a good chance you'll get to the top of the mountain—because of your experience, you can read the forest's trail markers, decipher the weather signs, and understand your body's signals as you work to conserve your energy during the climb up the mountain. But if you're a novice in the ways of the forest and if you're new to mountain climbing, you're going to need a guide to lead you up the mountain the first few times.

Knowledge management is geared toward the experienced woodsman moving through an intellectual forest. E-learning is geared toward people who don't have enough experience to tackle the intellectual forest on their own—they need a guide (instructor) and step-by-step instructions.

You can see that knowledge management and e-learning overlap, but they are aimed at different people with different experience levels.

1-14. Is e-learning something completely new?

❏ E-learning fits into a long tradition of learning at a distance.

Tell Me More

Learning at a distance is not new. That's what correspondence courses do. That's what "how to" books do. That's what public television programs at 5:30 A.M. do.

Apprenticeships, classroom courses, books, and correspondence courses were the way everyone learned until the flood of new technologies began in the middle of the twentieth century. From the 1960s onward, we've quickly seen the technology proceed through:

❏ Video courses (on tape or private TV network)
❏ Audiotape courses
❏ Computer-based, self-paced training (text-based)
❏ Computer-based, self-paced training (with multimedia)
❏ E-learning via the Internet

A key thing to note here is that the newer technologies don't usually replace the older technologies—instead, they build on top of them. So it's quite natural to see interactive courses on the Internet being used right alongside classroom courses or even blended together with classroom modules.

1-15. Where can you find out more about e-learning?

❑ Your best bet is to finish reading the rest of this book.
❑ Or, you can look on the Internet. There are hundreds of place to look, but you can start by looking at only a handful of Web sites.

Tell Me More

I've tried to keep this chapter short—as well as keeping the entire book short—but there is much, much more about e-learning you can find elsewhere. (This book is only a survival guide, not an encyclopedia of everything you can possibly know about e-learning.)

The best place to start learning more about e-learning is the Internet itself (just as you can find lots about almost anything on the Internet).

I recommend you start by looking at this handful of Web sites on the Internet:

❑ www.ibm.com/services/learning
❑ www.ibm.com/mindspan
❑ www.masie.com
❑ www.learnativity.com
❑ www.internettime.com/e.htm

These are certainly not the only sites—there are dozens of others. If you have a spare weekend or so, it might be fun to surf all over the Internet and look at as many of them as you can. How do you find more sites? Use a search engine to look for these words and phrases:

❑ e-learning
❑ elearning

❑ distance learning
❑ distributed learning

For example, if you want some advice on ROI for e-learning, use your favorite search engine to search for "e-learning ROI" and see what comes back. Then search for "distance learning ROI" and "distributed learning ROI." (If you don't have a favorite search engine, try www.google.com.)

Finally, you can look in bookstores for e-learning books. They might be categorized as e-learning books, distance learning books, or distributed learning books. You can also search for such books at the Internet bookstores like amazon.com, borders.com, and barnesandnoble.com.

Chapter Summary

E-learning is learning that uses computer technology, usually via the Internet.

❑ E-learning enables employees to learn at their work computer witout traveling to a classroom.
❑ E-learning lets your employees learn at a distance, over the Internet. For example, salespersons can get real-time training on new products without traveling out of the field.
❑ E-learning can be a scheduled session with an instructor and other students, or it can be an on-demand course that the employees can take for self-directed learning at a time when it's convenient.

E-learning can help your business so that:

❑ Employees can learn without traveling to class—the training is delivered right to their computers. This means that you can save on travel costs and that employees don't have to be away from work for extended periods of time.
❑ Employees can learn at their convenience—many e-learning courses don't have rigid start and end times. Many people can learn much better when they can learn at a convenient time.
❑ Employees can sometimes learn in ways that are more

effective than what they see in the traditional company classroom. Many people can learn better when the material to be learned is in bite-size pieces or spread over several weeks instead of packed into a couple of intensive days.

❑ Companies can get more bang for their education buck—especially when you can reduce existing expenses associated with going to class and when you structure e-learning to take advantage of its strengths.

The e-learning approach you take will depend on understanding what your learning situation really is, from a business point of view, and then tailoring e-learning to meet the needs of that situation

Research shows that e-learning works as well as classroom learning. You can use e-learning to teach almost anything that a business needs to teach. (But some things can be more effective when done in a classroom environment.)

It's safe to say that, in the long term, from five to ten years, all companies are good candidates for using e-learning. In the short term, from right now to a year or so from now, you have to think about whether your company's training situations are a good fit with the strengths of e-learning.

All this doesn't mean that e-learning is a silver bullet for all your training needs. Implementing e-learning in a simplistic or thoughtless way will probably not get you the benefits you're looking for. But if you go about it thoughtfully, you will most likely find that e-learning can fulfill its promise of giving your company a better-trained workforce.

CHAPTER TWO

Let's Be Specific—
Some E-Learning
Case Studies

> FIRST CITIZEN: "How apply you this?"
> —William Shakespeare's *Coriolanus*

E-learning is a single word but it doesn't refer to a single "thing." Instead, the word e-learning refers to a wide range of business training situations and a wide range of specific solutions. This chapter describes nearly a dozen case studies that show you:

❑ The range of "where you can use e-learning" in a business setting

❑ The range of different solutions that can all be called e-learning

Don't Read This Chapter!

That's right—don't read this chapter.

For now, just scan the table on the next page. You'll see that it lists several e-learning case studies (in no particular order) about applying e-learning to some typical situations that occur in businesses.

Yes, I realize that nearly a dozen case studies are a lot to contemplate at first. But the point I want you to see is that e-learning

29

can be applied to a number of different business training situations and that the e-learning solutions can range widely (all over the map, as it were).

To be specific, here's what you should do *instead of reading this chapter:*

1. Find one or two case studies in the table on the next page that match a current training situation in your business.

2. Turn to those case studies and read them.

3. Go on to Chapter 3 and keep reading the rest of the book.

Summary of Case Studies in This Chapter

E-Learning Case Study	Purpose
1. Product sales update training	Train salespeople in many countries around the world on your new product so they can start selling right away.
2. Technical certification training	Provide ongoing training for hundreds of company engineers so they maintain their technical certification.
3. Professional competency training	Train hundreds of employees on company-defined skills competencies such as project management, consulting, IT system administration.
4. Business tools training	Train hundreds of employees on new business tools that they are required to use on their jobs.
5. Technical skills training	Train hundreds of employees on-demand for technical skills like Java programming, data mining, databases, and so on.

E-Learning Case Study	Purpose
6. *"Ongoing professional" training*	Provide on-demand training to hundreds of employees in such professional skills as negotiating, running meetings, coaching, team dynamics, and so on.
7. *New salesperson training in "how to sell"*	Train dozens of brand-new salespeople each year—these new salespeople have never been in a sales job before.
8. *New-hire training*	Train dozens of new employees each year on what they need to know to be productive, contributing parts of your company.
9. *New HR benefits training*	Train your entire employee population, around the world, on a new health-benefit plan for your company.
10. *Informal technical seminars*	Communicate leading-edge research via informal seminars.
11. *Legal compliance training*	Train hundreds of employees at several locations on government regulations and laws on such topics as sexual harassment, workplace diversity, and so on

Note: Bookmark this page because many of the question/answer sections in the rest of this book will refer back to these case studies.

Case Study 1. Product Sales Update Training

You are the VP of Sales for Amalgamated Widgets, Inc., a multinational company that sells high-tech widgets as subcomponents in other high tech products. You have 800 salespeople in 20 countries all over the world, and you are getting ready for a major product launch.

Your new *Red Widget 1100* product line will be available in a month, replacing the *Blue Widget 1000* series of product. The *Blue Widget 1000* has been the main product line for the last year-and-a-half. The *Red Widget 1100* line has new underlying technology, faster speeds, and a more competitive price/performance ratio. Keeping your salespeople up to speed is crucial because your high-tech product line evolves every six to twelve months—this is the demanding pace set by high-tech competition.

All 800 salespeople are already experienced in selling the existing Blue Widget line of products, but they need to get up to speed quickly on the new Red Widget line. You want them to be selling effectively immediately after product launch.

You don't have to teach your salespeople about basic sales or even how to sell into your market. They are experienced sales personnel. What you do have to teach them is the new *Red Widget 1100* product characteristics (features and functions; feeds and speeds) and what new opportunities for sales the new product features open up.

You expect that the next generation of *Yellow Widget 1200* products will be available in nine to twelve months, so you have to maximize your opportunity to sell *Red Widget 1100's* in that short time window.

What's at Stake?

Your company has a lot riding on the revenue from the new *Red Widget 1100* products. You have a short time window in which to make the product sales. Any salesman who's not completely up to speed is going to cost your company revenue. Training your salespeople on the new product line is critical to your company's success. This is not something to do in a half-hearted way.

Student Motivation

The salespeople will be motivated to learn about the new Red Widget product because their salary depends directly on how well they will sell that new line.

That, however, is not the whole story. These are salespeople after all—and successful salespeople like to be "out selling," not "in learning about new products." You will still have to create the learning event to fit into the unique characteristics of the sales personnel (who are very different from technical personnel, management personnel, etc.). And you will still have to make sure that everyone gets the training. We all know how certain types of salespersons just like to "wing it," even if they are less effective when they do it that way.

Note: Stop a moment and think of your own e-learning solution before reading on.

Solution Factors

The critical components of this training are that:

> **W**hen the business stakes are high and you have lots of revenue riding on the training success, you need to emphasize training speed and also emphasize making sure everyone is actually trained to the level you want.

❑ Everyone gets trained in a short period of time.
❑ The training is fitted to the salesperson style (not to the technical person style, or the manager-type style). This essentially comes down to the fact that salespersons are people-oriented and are not typically the type to study on their own. Some kind of person-to-person contact (even if virtual) needs to be a part of the solution.

A good approach is to imitate what you would do if all the salespeople worked out of the same city. You'd bring them all in for a live seminar and complete the "training update" in a couple of hours with a series of presentations.

But with e-learning, you can do that in a virtual manner—you can run a virtual sales seminar over the Internet. You could have product experts and senior sales managers lecture on the new product features and explain how each feature affects the sales equation. You might also present some sales case studies for the new product that show how best to sell it. And you could give a short quiz at the end just to be sure that everyone understood the main points.

Webcasts are sometimes used for this type of live learning event, but I think it's even more effective to use Web lectures. The difference is that a Webcast depends heavily on the video transmission and often focuses on the "talking head" instead of the information being transmitted. That's good for a casual lecture, and for entertainment, but not when you really expect people to learn and remember critical facts.

Web lectures broadcast PowerPoint-type slides over the Internet with an audio voice-over. This means that each slide appears one by one on the computer screen, and you hear the lecturer talking about each slide. So you're sending the information by eye and by ear at the same time. With the Web lectures, you keep the focus on the slides and not on the person talking.

> **W**hen students are motivated because the training has a direct impact on whether they can continue doing their job, the training situation has a great chance of overall success.

Depending on the type of high-tech product you're selling, you might be able to do a good demo of the new product features over the Web so the salespeople can see it work even if they can't actually touch it. Don't spend too much energy fretting over this, however, because useful product demos are very hard to pull off (even at a live event). You could wind up spending all your energy on a marginally useful demo and neglect the more important content of the Web lectures.

Here are three other elements that will be critical to successful learning taking place for this case study:

1. You can have the salespeople ask questions and get answers during the session by using "voice technology over the Internet," a simultaneous telephone call with all participants, or an instant-messaging feature that lets all participants type questions and get instant text responses.

2. You can put the "product facts" at a Web site so salespeople can download them later (reference material for actual sales calls). This is the electronic equivalent of the binder full of handouts you'd get at a live session. You'll have to show how to use this reference Web site during the lecture part of the session.

3. You can use a short "quiz" (delivered over the Internet) to check that each salesperson actually attended the session and in fact learned enough about the new product. (You'll also need a way for salespeople to recover when they fail the quiz— you'd like to think that everyone will pass the quiz, but that will never be the case.)

Avoid structuring the training session in a way that is more appropriate to technical personnel instead of sales personnel. Salespeople want to know enough to sell the product, and that's often all they want to know.

Case Study 2. Technical Certification Training

You're the certification compliance officer for Acme Control Company. Your company employs 1,000 engineers who work at power plants all over the world.

Your engineers are certified by an outside agency to work on power plants. They can perform their work only if they continue to be recertified by that agency each year. There is a yearly test each engineer must pass.

It takes several months of training to certify a new engineer, but only a week of training to maintain an engineer's certification. You are interested in making sure that none of your already certified engineers fail the test.

In summary, the characteristics of the case study are that:

❑ You have engineers in many geographical areas.

❑ They all need to maintain their certification in order to keep doing their jobs.

❑ Constant training is accepted by the engineers to prepare to pass each year's certification exam.

❑ The engineers are motivated to keep up with their training.

What's at Stake?

You've had several engineers lose their certifications in past years, and you know from experience that it is very expensive in both time and money to replace them. You can lose contracts, and thus revenue, if a key engineer loses his certification.

Student Motivation

Your engineers are very motivated to keep their certification since they know their jobs depend on it.

Note: Stop a moment and think of your own e-learning solution before reading on.

Solution Factors

The solution approach here probably centers on a learning management system (LMS) that will manage the overall training program in an automated way. (Chapter 9 describes more about such learning management systems.)

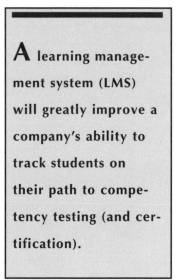

A learning management system (LMS) will greatly improve a company's ability to track students on their path to competency testing (and certification).

First, you developed a series of training courses that the engineers can take on demand over the Internet at their convenience. These courses will probably give the engineers "bite-size" chunks of training so they can fit them in among their other duties.

- ❑ Much of the training can be designed as self-study chunks of training, so that the engineer can do it at a time that's convenient for her work schedule.
- ❑ But other parts can be a virtual classroom experience with an instructor and a couple of dozen students gathered together at the same time in a virtual place on the Internet. The main reason you might only do a few of these virtual classroom sessions is the scheduling problem of getting everyone together at the same exact time.

The learning management system will then present the "roadmap" of courses that each engineer needs to complete. The LMS will track which courses the engineer has taken and which are still to be taken to keep up with the certification training. In fact, the LMS can automatically schedule students for classes and can even automatically prompt the student with an e-mail when she's falling behind.

The learning management system will also deliver quizzes and practice certification tests that prove that the engineer has absorbed the training. And, perhaps most importantly, the LMS will provide reports to you (the certification compliance officer) and to other authorized management about which engineers are on track for recertification.

As alternatives to that solution,

- ❏ Your e-learning courses might include courses with a remote instructor as well as self-directed training. The instructor, even at a distance over the Internet, will help motivate the students and help them learn more effectively.
- ❏ In addition to the training courses themselves, you might want a Web site that acts as an "online library" of reference materials for certification. This online library could be used during the courses, but it could also be referred to during the engineer's actual work.

A critical element of making this successful is making it easy to track which engineers are on track and which are falling behind. For example, sending computer-based training to each engineer on a CD-ROM wouldn't work if you couldn't tell which engineers were keeping up with their training and which were falling behind.

Case Study 3. Professional Competency Training

You're a VP at Virtual Nuts & Bolts, a multinational conglomerate that owns companies involved in a number of different businesses, from manufacturing to high-tech management consulting, to e-business software.

Virtual Nuts & Bolts has company-defined competencies (also called "in-house certifications") for positions like:

❑ Project Managers
❑ IT System Administrators
❑ Consultants
❑ … and so on

Employees are expected to pass company-defined competency exams in order to perform those jobs. For example, new project managers need to be certified within three years in order to continue in the project management job. You have hundreds of employees on track to pass their competency exams.

Note: The case study here is similar to Case Study #2 above, but there are a couple of key differences for this case study:

1. *This is a company-defined competency (or certification). An outside group will not be shutting your business down if some of your people fail the certification exam.*

2. *You can continue to have employees performing the job even before they are certified. And you can choose to have them continue to perform the job even if they fail the exam. (Although you probably don't want them doing it for long if they continue failing the exam.)*

3. *You are not bound to meet a deadline set by an outside regulatory organization—for example, you don't have a yearly recertification that you must meet. You can be more flexible about the time limits within which all the training and exams must be completed.*

What's at Stake?

At stake is your ability to get high performance from your employees in certain jobs—where passing the competency exam is the mark of a certain skill level. You expect your business to run more productively when these key jobs are staffed to a predefined skill level.

But, the stakes are not as high as in Case Study #2 where the certification was required by an outside organization. There, your business could be shut down. In this case study, your business performance might be degraded if employees have not passed their exams, but it will not grind to a halt.

Student Motivation

Your employees are motivated to do the training and pass their competency tests, but they are not quite as motivated as the engineers in Case Study #2. There, the engineers could immediately lose their jobs if they didn't pass the recertification exam every year. In this case study, the pressure is not as intense so the employees might not be as motivated to be faithful to a training schedule. Their jobs depend on it in the long run, but not in the short run.

Note: Stop a moment and think of your own e-learning solution before reading on.

Solution Factors

The solution approach here, much like the one in Case Study #2, is centered on a learning management system (LMS). You need the LMS to manage the overall training program. You could never keep track of all the employees and how far they've progressed if you had to do it manually.

The first step is to develop a collection of training courses that lead your employees to the expected skill level. Depending on the type of competency being taught, the courses might be completely self-directed online, or you might include some courses with collaboration and instructors. In some cases (depending on the subject matter), you might even need to have a face-to-face session in addition to the online courses. We call this "blending" the instruction, and you'll remember that the IBM management development training course described in Chapter 1 did it this way because there were training situations that need face-to-face interaction.

Then, you need the exams that the employees will have to pass.

The learning management system will present the "roadmap" of courses that each employee on a path to a competency exam needs to complete to prep for certification. The LMS will track which courses the employee has taken and which are still to be taken.

Some LMSs can automatically schedule students for classes and can even automatically prompt the student with an e-mail when he's falling behind. And the learning management system will also deliver the quizzes and tests that move the employee along the competency roadmap, as well as delivering the final competency exam online.

The LMS will also provide reports to company management about where the various employees are in their competency road map, and it will report on who passed the final exams. The LMS can sometimes manage "testing out" of certain courses. If an employee has previous job experience, it would be useful to let the employee "test out" of taking the class.

> **Y**ou'd be surprised how often business situations require making sure that every member in a group learns something, and that each one learns it by a deadline

The key advantage you have in this case study is motivated students. When the training is clearly connected to keeping a job, your training program has a good chance of overall success.

Case Study 4. Business Tools Training

You're the sales manager for Ace Products, Inc., and you've just purchased new handheld Internet devices for your 400 salespeople nationwide. The key application on the new handheld device is the sales tracking application. Salespeople will input data about each sales call, and upload it to the central server at the end of the day. Management can then run a variety of sales reports on the daily sales data.

The handheld devices are being shipped to each salesperson this week. By the end of the month, you expect to start pulling management reports.

What's at Stake?

This real-time sales information system is critical to your business. But you won't be successful in getting that data unless each salesperson can work the handheld Internet device correctly and run the sales call application properly. Bad data would be worse than no data.

Student Motivation

Most salespeople will want to learn how to use the new handheld devices properly, but many of them will try to just "wing it." Others will not be interested in using the device at all until a specific sales situation forces them to use it to close some business.

Note: Stop a moment and think of your own e-learning solution before reading on.

> **Y**our learning problem might be critical in a tactical timeframe, or it might be something that is solved only in the strategic timeframe.

Solution Factors

The critical success factors here are that:

1. Each salesperson needs to take the training.
2. You need to know that each salesperson has minimum skills with the new device.
3. And you need to complete all this in a short period of time.

One solution approach is to create a self-directed training course that each salesperson can take at her own convenience through a Web browser. (It would be very difficult to get everyone together for a scheduled session, even if you had a main session and several make-up sessions.) This will be a one- to two-hour training session that teaches people how to use the handheld device for sales tracking via simulated sales case studies. Doing the training via case studies will keep the salesperson's interest and will show her exactly how the device fits into the real work environment.

Supplementing this main training will be a Web page with FAQs and an e-mail address where salespeople can address specific questions and get an answer within a day.

The last part of the solution is probably the most important. Each salesperson will be required to complete a short online quiz by a certain date to prove that she's taken the training and has attained at least the minimum skill level. This will also serve you as a reporting mechanism so you can tell who didn't bother with the training.

Case Study 5. Technical Skills Training

You are the HR manager for MultiPRODUCTS Inc, a medium-size company with 10,000 employees working in the high-tech services market.

Many of your employees are highly skilled in their specific area of expertise, but their technical breadth is often lacking. For example, you've found that many of your C++ programmers are deficient in networking and in database skills. Your UNIX system administrators are poor at understanding data mining. And all your administrative people could do better with spreadsheets.

What's at Stake?

The training situation here is not immediately critical to your business. You'd certainly like to have everyone better trained in these technical areas—it would probably help things runs a lot more smoothly and efficiently in your business. But if they don't, your business will keep going nonetheless. This case study falls into the category of a "strategically good thing to do as long as it's not going to cost too much in the short term."

It's important to distinguish this case study from Case Studies #2 and #3 on certification-type training. In those cases the training needs were indeed critical to the business in a fixed time period.

Student Motivation

Your employees will have good intentions for taking courses outside their immediate job responsibilities, but they will have lots of business pressures that hinder many of them from acting on those good intentions. (Think of this in terms of the good intentions people have when they start an exercise program, weight loss program, etc. Or just think of your New Year's resolutions from last year.) Your employees will need strong motivations from your management team to keep working on skills that are not immediately important to their day-to-day job responsibilities.

Note: Stop a moment and think of your own e-learning solution before reading on.

Solution Factors

The solution approach you take here will depend on how important the different technical skills are to your company. The skill set will divide into (A) moderately important technical skills, and (B) critical skills. (There's also the case of "unimportant skills" but you probably wouldn't even want to try to address those.) You might want different solutions for each of Cases A and B:

Case A

Moderately important technical skills. For this case you offer self-directed, on-demand training to these students, and you should probably try to buy this standard training from industry vendors instead of creating it yourself. If you are currently sending these students to class, this will result in an immediate savings in travel costs. Part of the solution must also include a tracking and reward mechanism for students who complete e-learning courses. They need to get credit on their human resources record for completing the courses.

Case B

Critically important technical skills. For this case, you might offer more elaborate e-learning. You might include here virtual classroom training with a remote instructor, and even e-lab training where students can access hands-on labs over the Internet. This approach will probably cost more, but if the skills are genuinely important to your company, it will be money well spent. Just as in Case A, part of the solution also must include a tracking and reward mechanism for students who complete e-learning courses. They at least need to get credit on their human resources record for completing the courses.

Since most of what you need in this category of training is already created by industry vendors, you don't want to create your own courseware here. And you want to avoid anything here that costs too much.

Depending on how important the training is to your business, you might want to track which students complete which courses. However, you can't put yourself in the position of punishing employees for not completing this kind of training.

Case Study 6. "Ongoing Professional" Skills Training

You are the CEO of Worldwide E-Consultants, a services company specializing in all manner of IT computer services and consulting. You have 3,000 employees at seven different locations in six time zones.

Many of your employees, although not your key employees, were recruited primarily for their technical skills with the hopes that their professional skills would grow on the job. But you've noticed that many of the rough edges are not smoothing out just by working on the job. As a consequence, you're setting up a new policy that requires each employee to complete five days of "professional" training each year in such topics as:

- ❏ Negotiating
- ❏ Leadership
- ❏ Business Issues
- ❏ Teamwork
- ❏ Running meetings

What's at Stake?

The training case study here is similar to Case Study #5 in that it's important to your business, but it's not critical. You'd like to have everyone better trained in these professional areas. But your business will continue at roughly current levels in the short term if your employees don't improve their professional-type skills. Again, this case study falls into the category of a "strategically good thing to do" as long as it's not going to cost too much.

Student Motivation

Your employees will have good intentions, but they will also need a job requirement like completing five days of this training every year. That five-day requirement is the key to the student motivation. What happens to the employees who meet the requirement? What happens to those who don't?

> **Y**ou don't have to create your own e-learning courseware if you can buy it from industry vendors.

Note: Stop a moment and think of your own e-learning solution before reading on.

Solution Factors

As in Case Study #5, a good solution approach here is to offer self-directed, on-demand training to these students. The students can take the e-learning courses on their own at their convenience. You should try to buy this standard training from industry vendors instead of creating it yourself.

If you are currently sending employees to classroom courses for this sort of training, on-demand e-learning will result in an immediate savings in travel costs. A critical element of the solution must also include a tracking mechanism for students who complete e-learning courses. They need to get credit on their human resources record for completing the courses.

To help with student motivation, you could set up the e-learning solution so that you have a threaded discussion Web page for students taking the same course at roughly the same time. Students can leave messages at the page for others to respond to. In addition, you can involve a mentor or instructor in these message-based discussions.

And you should think of other rewards for faithful students.

Case Study 7. New Salesperson Training in "How to Sell"

You are the sales manager of Really Kool Hardware Products, and you hire at least fifty to sixty salespersons each year who need training in the basics of "how to sell." This is not just training in "how to sell your company's products" but training in basic sales techniques. These new employees are generally college graduates in computer science with sales potential but no sales experience and no demonstrable sales skills.

What Are the Stakes?

Your company's revenues depend on getting these new salespeople fully up to speed and out selling. A new-hire salesperson can't drive revenue for your company until he knows the minimum about selling. It's also important to find as early as possible those who aren't cut out for a career in sales.

Student Motivation

The new salespersons are very motivated to do this training because they know their job depends on it. If they don't learn how to be a salesperson, they won't have a job.

Note: Stop a moment and think of your own e-learning solution before reading on.

Solution Factors

You could construct a four-part sales e-learning class like this:

Part 1: Knowledge of Sales Basics. This is self-directed, on-demand training delivered via the Web, with tracking and a quiz for each course module. This is useful for information transfer, but it doesn't do much for sales skills. And you're going to need a skilled salesperson who knows how to do it, not just a person who is knowledgeable about sales theory.

Part 2: Sales Case Studies. An interim step for gaining sales skills is a series of collaborative sessions with other new persons at different locations all over the company. In virtual teams, and with an experienced instructor to guide them, the new salespersons will take up sales case studies, figure out answers as a team, and present the responses online to the instructor. All of this will happen over the Internet.

Part 3: Face-to-Face Sessions. The next step is for the sales students to participate in face-to-face sessions with an instructor in order to learn the one-on-one sales techniques. (If such face-to-face sessions are impossible to organize, this can be conducted over the Internet as well, but it needs to be either one-on-one sessions or very small teams of students.)

Part 4: Ongoing Mentoring. The final step is for an experienced salesperson to be assigned to each salesperson to act as a mentor for a couple of months. This mentoring can occur via e-mail, via instant messaging, or by phone.

> **"S**kills" are different from "knowledge." It's one thing to know all about the physics of swinging a baseball bat, but it's another thing altogether to hit home runs off major league pitching.

Instead of having the student display his new sales skills face to face, you could have the student videotape himself and send several of those for instructor critique. With a low-cost PC camera, it might even be done over the Web.

Key to making this work is keeping the focus on the skills taught in Parts 2 and 3, instead of on the knowledge covered in Part 1. Selling is a skill, and it is not enough to "know about" sales theory and product facts. It's one thing to know all about the physics of swinging a baseball bat, but it's another thing altogether to hit home runs off major league pitching.

Case Study 8. New-Hire Training

You are the HR manager of We-Do-Lots-of-Important-Stuff, Inc., and your company hires about 700 new employees each year—about half directly from college and about half as professional hires with related job experience. Most of these employees will be mobile workers, and you will seldom see them in a company office. Each employee needs to learn the basics of working in your company. They need to know about policies, procedures, sources of information, etc. For example, each new employee needs to learn how to fill out an expense account and select benefits options.

What's at Stake?

The stakes are the morale of the new hires. They can limp along without any training, but you need to have them feel comfortable in their new company. Employee morale is directly related to employee productivity and turnover.

Student Motivation

The new hires will initially be very interested in this training, but as their job pressures increase, they will be inclined to take only that training that's immediately applicable to their day-to-day responsibilities.

Note: Stop a moment and think of your own e-learning solution before reading on.

Solution Factors

The solution approach here could center on having the new hire take a lot of self-directed training, which could be tracked to ensure completion, and then putting the new hire in touch with a mentor.

You can use self-directed, on-demand e-learning that the new hire can take online through a Web browser. The student can learn company history, company policies, and also things like sexual harassment and health and safety issues. Part of this solution is also a virtual library of key policy and procedure documents, so the new hire can go back to a Web page and get reference documents at a later time.

You might want to include "self-check quizzes" so the new hires can tell what they've learned. You want to avoid too much emphasis on tracking and quizzing of the new hires. You don't want to turn off your employees by making them take quizzes that they can't always pass. Remember that the real goal is to get each new hire to feel comfortable so they can be more productive sooner.

You also want to avoid the complete lack of a human touch. You can build in the human feeling with mentors, occasional face-to-face sessions, collaborative online sessions with new hires, or other personalized communications with the employee.

Furthermore, you probably want a tracking system that shows whether the new hires actually completed the training, and you might want some short quizzes to determine whether they are actually learning or just turning the Web pages.

Another important part to new hire training is to assign a mentor to each new hire. This mentor should be an experienced employee who communicates with the new hire by e-mail or by phone—the mentor and the new hire do not need to be at the same physical location.

You also might want to consider the following:

❑ You can get courses on standard business issues (like sexual harassment, health and safety, etc.) from industry vendors. You do not need to create your own.

❑ A Web page with frequently asked questions (FAQs) for new hires is a nice touch, as is a help line that's answered by a knowledgeable human being. Sometimes a new hire will need to talk to someone in person.

Case Study 9. New HR Benefits Training

You are the HR manager for CrescendoForte, Inc., a management consulting firm with 4,000 consultants working at consulting engagements with clients at geographic locations all around the world.

You have been negotiating with several healthcare providers over the past six months to improve the healthcare benefits for CrescendoForte's employees. Negotiations have been successful, and the new healthcare plan is going to take effect in three months.

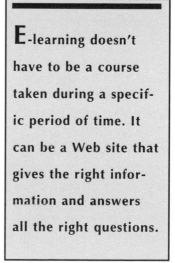

E-learning doesn't have to be a course taken during a specific period of time. It can be a Web site that gives the right information and answers all the right questions.

During that three-month time period, employees need to choose from a menu of healthcare options that will determine their level of coverage in all manner of healthcare problems. You have had the same healthcare plan for the past ten years, and the new one, while less costly to the company overall, requires that each employee make a number of choices that are significantly different from the old healthcare plan.

Employees will need training in the specific details of the new healthcare plan so that each person can make a good choice.

What's at Stake?

The stakes are employee morale for your entire employee population. Rolling out a new HR benefits package can damage employee morale if the employees feel they didn't get a fair chance at making the benefits choices that would be most advantageous to each of them.

Student Motivation

The employees will be very interested in learning about the new benefits package since it is of immediate personal interest to each employee. They will not, however, be willing to take lengthy training modules.

Note: Stop a moment and think of your own e-learning solution before reading on.

Solution Factors

One good e-learning solution for this case study would be to create a Web site about the new healthcare benefits plan; part of that Web site would be short training modules that an employee can select on demand. Any e-learning training module in this environment should be very short. A lengthy course that lasts more than ten or fifteen minutes will cause people to start drifting away. Aim for short training modules of ten minutes or less.

The actual training solution is only a small part of communicating the new benefits plan to your employees. In addition to the short, ten-minute training modules, the Web site can have a wealth of reference information:

- ❑ Handy facts about the new plan
- ❑ Differences from the old plan
- ❑ Case studies showing how different people might take advantage of the plan
- ❑ Frequently asked questions (FAQs) and answers

You can think of the information at this Web site as the virtual equivalent of the hardcopy booklet that you would have sent each employee in the past, with the added benefit of e-learning training modules. From the Web site the employees always have access to the information, the information can always be up-to-date with the last-minute changes, and it doesn't get lost like so many of the hardcopy booklets used to.

The key point for the learning case study is that you're not starting at ground zero with most employees when talking about healthcare plans. They already know a lot—what they don't know is what's different and how it might affect each of them. Your short training modules might focus on "what's different."

Another important part of the training solution would be a help desk that can answer questions by phone or e-mail. For something like healthcare benefits, employees often want to talk to a human being.

Some other things to include in this solution are that:

- ❑ You need to be sure that the employee can print out all the important information. Some people just work better with information on paper, and some might need to take the information away from the computer. Most browsers let you print tolerably well, but there are ways of constructing Web pages so they don't print well at all. Be careful.
- ❑ You might want a calculator tool on the Web site that lets the employee try different "what if" case studies for different benefits options.

Finally, there's no need to test the employees on their knowledge and certainly no need to report on how well they've learned the information.

Case Study 10. Informal Technical Seminars

You are the head of research for ChemCALResearch Associates, a chemical research firm with about 1,500 chemists and chemical engineers at five research locations in three time zones. Your training goal is to communicate leading-edge research among all your chemists. This is beyond the communications that happen in formal scientific publications. You're aiming for something more informal and much more timely. What you want is for researchers to present their research approaches and results to their peer chemists, so that the state-of-the-art information will flow quickly through the organization and improve your competitive advantage.

Your training problem would be very much simplified if all the chemists were physically located at the same facility. In that case, you could hold regular lunch-and-learn seminars. Interested chemists could walk over and hear a seminar when it covered a topic they were interested in. But with several research facilities in different locations and time zones, you need a different approach. Chemists cannot just fly off to a live seminar over lunch.

What Are the Stakes?

The stakes are the speed with which "state-of-the-art research information" flows through your company. By quickly spreading fresh research approaches and promising results throughout your organization, you can get more brainpower behind new ideas. And since such research information is the key thing your company produces, this is critical to your business success.

Student Motivation

Every chemist in your company will not be interested in every seminar. But when the seminar topic touches on what a particular chemist is working on, the interest will be intense.

Note: Stop a moment and think of your own e-learning solution before reading on.

Solution Factors

The key to making this kind of informal training a success is to imitate the informal lunch-and-learn event you would have run if everyone worked at the same location. What you need is a way to do a seminar in a self-service way so that chemists will be motivated to give such seminars without making too much of a project of it. If it's too hard to do, the chemist will just continue working on her mainline chemical research and not bother to give a seminar.

Think of what a lunch-and-learn event would be like: The chemist would prepare a couple of overhead transparencies (or do it in PowerPoint) and then stand up in front of the group and give an informal talk.

The key success factors are:

1. Can the chemist do it herself?

2. Can she do it quickly?

3. Can it be up and running almost immediately after the PowerPoint slides are uploaded and the audio recording is done?

You want to avoid anything that makes it hard for the chemist to quickly construct her own presentation. And you want to avoid anything that delays getting the recorded seminar up and running on the Web for your other employees. In other words, can you keep that same level of self-service and informality and still deliver it over the Internet? Yes, you can.

The technology exists (IBM calls them "Web lectures") for the chemist to prepare a handful of PowerPoint slides, upload them to a Web server, call a number on the phone and record the voice-over for each slide, and then, within a matter of hours, have the recorded seminar available for delivery over the Web. Being recorded for replay, the seminar can be accessed on demand—whenever any of the peer chemists needs to look at it. If you then add in an electronic registration capability so you know who attended each seminar, you have the Internet equivalent of lunch-and-learn seminars.

Some solution alternatives:

- ❏ You could record a video of the chemist talking about her topic and transmit that over the Internet. The technology exists for small PC cameras to record informal talks. The danger here is that without a professional cameraman, the focus will be on the talking head instead of on the information. In other words, nonprofessional camerawork can be distracting.
- ❏ You could run live lunch-and-learn events at one location, record them with a camera crew, and replay them over the Internet for the other locations.

Case Study 11. Legal Compliance Training

You are the HR manager for Consolidated Call Centers, Inc., and your company outsources call centers for other businesses around the world. You have 5,000 call-center employees in seventy-five different locations. You need to train the call-center employees on a number of legal compliance issues such as sexual harassment, bribery, corruption, privacy, and diversity.

You can't pull the employees away from the phones to participate in face-to-face seminars on these legal compliance topics, but you still need to ensure that all your employees understand the laws and regulations that govern the workplace.

What Are the Stakes?

The stakes are twofold:

1. To improve the employee work environment
2. To show evidence of good faith training in the event of lawsuits

Student Motivation

Student motivation will be mixed. Some employees will be interested in some of the legal compliance topics, but others will not be. For legal reasons, you need to make sure that everyone is trained on these topics regardless of whether they are motivated to learn it.

Note: Stop a moment and think of your own e-learning solution before reading on.

Solution Factors

A good solution here is to use self-directed online courses that let your call-center employees take the training at their computers, at their own pace, and at a time when it fits into their schedules. Employees should be able to take a bite-size training module that lasts ten or fifteen minutes, bookmark their places, and return to the call-center work.

A key component of the solution is to track each employee's completion of the online training. This is important because, in most cases, legal compliance means that 100 percent of the employee population completed the training. It isn't enough for an employee to start the training and just flip through it as fast as he can click a mouse.

You also might want to add self-check tests as a validation step.

Some things you probably want to avoid:

- ❏ Any solution that takes too much time at one sitting
- ❏ Any solution that hinders call-center employees from taking the training on demand at any convenient time
- ❏ Any solution that does not track who completed the training

Chapter Summary

E-learning is a single word but it doesn't refer to a single "thing." Instead, the word e-learning refers to a wide range of business training situations and a wide range of specific solutions. This chapter describes nearly a dozen case studies that show you:

- ❏ The range of applicability of e-learning in a business setting

❏   The range of different solutions that can all be called e-learning

These were the case studies covered in this chapter:

1. *Product Sales Update Training*
   Train salespeople in many countries around the world on your new product so they can start selling right away.

2. *Technical Certification Training*
   Provide ongoing training for hundreds of company engineers so they maintain their technical certification.

3. *Professional Competency Training*
   Train hundreds of employees on company-defined skills competencies such as project management, consulting, IT system administration.

4. *Business Tools Training*
   Train hundreds of employees on new business tools that they are required to use on their jobs.

5. *Technical Skills Training*
   Train hundreds of employees on-demand for technical skills like Java programming, data mining, databases, and so on.

6. *"Ongoing Professional" Skills Training*
   Provide on-demand training to hundreds of employees in such professional skills as negotiating, running meetings, coaching, team dynamics, and so on.

7. *New Salesperson Training in "How to Sell"*
   Train dozens of brand-new salespeople each year—these new salespeople have never been in a sales job before.

8. *New-Hire Training*
   Train dozens of new employees each year on what they need to know to be productive, contributing parts of your company.

9. *New HR Benefits Training*
   Train your entire employee population around the world on a new health-benefits plan for your company.

10. *Informal Technical Seminars*
Communicate leading-edge research via informal seminars.

11. *Legal Compliance Training*
Train hundreds of employees at several locations on government regulations and laws on such topics as sexual harassment, workplace diversity, and so on.

CHAPTER THREE

What Does E-Learning Cost?

DON PEDRO: "The fashion of the world is to avoid cost."
—William Shakespeare's *Much Ado About Nothing*

This chapter will give you a feel for how to think about e-learning costs. Understanding costs will help you make sound business decisions about using e-learning in your business. Your good business judgment will work here just as it does when you make any other business decision.

As a businessperson, you naturally think about e-learning as a business tool. I know, and I know you already know, that businesses need to get the "bang for the buck" from business tools, and e-learning is no different.

And I know how little patience you have for people who show you the glamour shots of an e-learning system without regard to balancing the cost versus the business value. You can't run a business with a justification of "See how wonderful that looks. Now give us lots of money to implement it."

Don't get me wrong—I believe that e-learning can usually be cost-justified. But that doesn't mean that all types of e-learning in all situations at all times are cost-justified for your business.

Questions and Answers in This Chapter

3-1. What does e-learning really cost?

3-2. What does the cost of an e-learning solution depend on?

3-3. What else affects the costs of e-learning?

3-4. How do you develop an ROI for e-learning?

3-5. How much confidence should you put in an ROI?

3-6. What are your make/buy elements for e-learning?

3-7. What do e-learning "solution providers" cost?

3-1. What does e-learning really cost?

❑ The costs for e-learning can vary widely, just as the costs of buying a car vary widely.

❑ You could spend hundreds, or you could spend multi-millions.

Tell Me More

One of the first questions I hear when I talk about e-learning to business managers is "What does e-learning really cost?" And the answer is always "It depends." (And my answer always receives a collective groan in reply.)

The following table gives you a ballpark look at what some e-learning solutions might cost. You can see from the table that it really does depend.

E-Learning Solution	Ballpark Cost
A single e-learning course with e-mail lessons ("correspondence course" with an instructor and a handful of students). No overall tracking and no automated testing.	Hundreds

E-Learning Solution	Ballpark Cost
A single self-study e-learning course to be delivered to a moderate number of students. No overall tracking, no automated testing.	Thousands
Dozens of instructor-led, interactive and collaborative e-learning courses, plus dozens of self-study courses delivered over the Internet to hundreds of students, with basic student tracking and automated testing.	Multithousands to millions
Corporate e-learning university with robust course catalog and learning management features for delivering hundreds of courses to thousands of students.	Millions

Clearly, as a businessperson you'd like to use the approach having the lowest cost. But that assumes that providing the lowest-cost approach can actually do the job you need to get done. You can get a used car for $500, but if you need to get from New York City to Paris, that used car won't do the complete job. (Right off, it will sink into the Atlantic Ocean as soon as you head east from Long Island.)

As a businessperson, you're already familiar with business expenses that can vary widely depending on what you're trying to accomplish. For example, what does it cost to buy a computer for your business? The first question is, What kind of computer are you trying to buy? Are you buying a laptop computer for light word processing and e-mail? Are you buying a network server as a key part of your corporate IT infrastructure? Are you buying a supercomputer as part of a scientific program to predict hurricanes? The costs of these different kinds of computers, too, range from hundreds to millions.

This is a good time to flip back to Chapter 2 and review some of the different situations in which a business can use e-learning. Some of the proposed solutions to those case studies can be accomplished at a relatively low cost, but others will require major investment. The table below gives you ballpark costs for the case studies from Chapter 2:

Note: I think it goes without saying that I'm not trying to be too precise here. Your actual costs will vary depending on the complexity of your solution and who's building it for you.

E-Learning Case Study[1]	Purpose	Ballpark Cost
1. *Product sales update training*	Train salespeople in many countries around the world on your new product so they can start selling right away.	Thousands
2. *Technical certification training*	Provide ongoing training for hundreds of company engineers so they maintain their technical certification.	Multi-thousands to millions
3. *Professional competency training*	Train hundreds of employees on company-defined skills competencies such as project management, consulting, IT system administration	Multi-thousands to millions
4. *Business tools training*	Train hundreds of employees on new business tools that they are required to use on their jobs.	Thousands
5. *Technical skills training*	Train hundreds of employees on-demand for technical skills like Java programming, data mining, databases, and so on.	Multi-thousands to millions
6. *"Ongoing professional" training*	Provide on-demand training to hundreds of employees in such professional skills as negotiating, running meetings, coaching, team dynamics, and so on	Multi-thousands to millions

E-Learning Case Study[1]	Purpose	Ballpark Cost
7. *New salesperson training in "how to sell"*	Train dozens of brand-new sales-people each year—these new sales people have never been in a sales job before	Multi-thousands
8. *New-hire training*	Train dozens of new employees each year on what they need to know to be productive, contributing parts of your company.	Thousands
9. *New HR benefits training*	Train your entire employee population, around the world, on a new health-benefits plan for your company.	Multi-thousands
10. *Informal technical seminars*	Communicate leading-edge research via informal seminars	Multi-thousands
11. *Legal compliance training*	Train hundreds of employees at several locations on government regulations and laws on such topics as sexual harassment, workplace diversity, and so on.	Multi-thousands

1. These case studies are described in detail in Chapter 2.

3-2. What does the cost of an e-learning solution depend on?

❑ The cost components for e-learning include the course-ware, the course delivery expenses (including instructors), marketing/promotional communications with the students, and administration and support expenses.

Tell Me More

You can make better business decisions about e-learning if you have a good grasp of what the cost components really are. (In the same way, knowing that the cost of owning a car is partly the purchase price but also includes the ongoing cost of maintenance and insurance helps you figure out what kind of car you can really afford to buy.)

In a sense, e-learning is a lot like any kind of product you're trying to get to a customer. You already know that the major costs for making and selling any product to a customer depend on:

❑ Making the product (or buying it to resell)
❑ Marketing it so your target customer knows how it meets a need that she has (and so the customer knows that you have the product available)
❑ Delivering it to the target customer
❑ Administration and support personnel for the previous tasks (often thought of as an indirect cost)

If you think of e-learning using that basic product model, with the student as the customer, then the basic e-learning cost components will turn out to be very familiar to you.

❑ It's going to cost you time and money to create (or buy) the e-learning courses.
❑ It's going to cost you time and money to make the students aware of the courses.
❑ It's going to cost you time and money to deliver the e-learning courses to the students.

The following table summarizes the cost factors for e-learning:

Cost Element	Comments
E-learning courseware	Course development cost (or cost of purchasing/renting existing vendor-developed courseware). Even if you have courseware designed for the classroom, it will cost you something to prepare it for e-learning use.

Cost Element	Comments
Course delivery	New hardware and software for your e-learning environment unless you're using computers and IT infrastructure that already exist in your company (and that are being paid for another way).
	Instructors, assuming your e-learning approach uses instructors.
Marketing communications to students	Promotional communications to the prospective students about the courses.
Administration and support	Administrative personnel to load courses, manage schedules, fix problems, etc. (Don't forget the user help desk.)

Your e-learning implementation might have additional incidental costs, but when you're doing a basic cost analysis, the table includes the main costs to look at.

3-3. What else affects the costs of e-learning?

❑ The biggest thing influencing your e-learning costs is the size and complexity of your training problem.
❑ There are only a handful of factors that make up the remaining dimensions you need to think about.

Tell Me More

Perhaps the biggest thing influencing your e-learning costs is the size of your problem. Think of it this way: If your problem is to move people from one end of the city to another, then you have a rough grasp of part of the problem. But it's a different problem altogether if you're trying to move a half-dozen people one time or if you're moving 100,000 people every day. In the first case, you can rent a van and drive them over yourself. In the second case, you might want to consider getting the city to build a rapid transit system.

There are only a handful of key factors that can affect the size and complexity of your e-learning problem and thus affect your e-learning costs. These problem factors are listed below, but you can find details about them in Chapter 8:

- ❑ Number of students
- ❑ Student time available for training
- ❑ Time to build
- ❑ Deadline to train everyone
- ❑ Long- versus short-term shelf life
- ❑ Starting and ending skill levels
- ❑ Need for instructor
- ❑ Need for collaboration

3-4. How do you develop an ROI for e-learning?

- ❑ You can't avoid risk, but doing a return on investment (ROI) analysis lets you quantify the risk.
- ❑ There are two types of ROI analysis you can do for e-learning:
  - ❑ Cost analysis: how it saves money (if you already have existing training you're running).
  - ❑ Value analysis: how it improves value (lets you do things you couldn't before).

Tell Me More

ROI is "return on investment." As a businessperson, ROI is what you spend your time figuring out day in and day out so you can make good business decisions. No organization has all the resources to do the things it would like to do. ROI analysis helps you figure out if you should spend money on project A, project B, or project C (or sometimes on more than one of them, or even none of them).

Your business is always faced with this situation: The roof is leaking, the kitchen needs remodeling, and the car is no longer getting the gas mileage it used to. And you don't have the money to fix all of those problems. (You never have enough money to do all the things you might do.) Which of those, if any, should you invest in?

You typically do what brings you the most return, the most benefit—where "benefit" might mean either getting something positive in return or avoiding something negative. Preventing water damage from a leaky roof is avoiding a negative consequence, but that might be the most important thing to do at the moment.

You've already seen from a previous question/answer section that there is a wide range of e-learning costs. You could spend only thousands on e-learning, or you could spend many millions. But if you're spending only thousands to get little or no benefit, then you're wasting your thousands. If you're spending millions to get multimillions in benefit, then you're spending your millions wisely.

The key insight is that "costs themselves are meaningless." It's the ROI that helps you determine whether something is a good deal. So much depends on the benefits you're trying to get for that cost.

There are two main ways of looking at an e-learning ROI calculation:

1. Cost-focused ROI—where your main concern is reducing existing expenses

2. Value-focused ROI—where your main concern is getting more value

These two approaches are not mutually exclusive. If you can, you should use both approaches and get an even fuller picture. We will, however, look at each one separately in the following sections:

Cost-Focused ROI

E-learning is immediately attractive to you if your business is already doing a great deal of training and you want to reduce costs. You might already be spending thousands or millions on training and you'd like to spend less. For example, recall the example of the IBM management development training in Chapter 1. In that case, shifting a major part, but not all, of the training from the classroom to an e-learning delivery dramatically reduced costs.

I'll be using "ducats" as the monetary unit for the ROI examples. I do this to underline the fact that the cost numbers I quote in this book are not supposed to be real. The ducat was a coin, usually of gold, used at various times in different European countries. (The first ducat was struck by Roger II of Sicily.)

Let's say you are planning to spend 1,000 ducats for training new managers this year in the traditional classroom manner, but you think that e-learning might be an improvement. Here's the general shape of a cost-focused ROI analysis. (Your numbers, of course, will vary based on your situation.)

Existing Cost for Classroom Training	Replace with E-Learning
Courseware update costs = 100 ducats	Courseware costs = 325 ducats
Communications costs = 25 ducats	Communications costs = 100 ducats
Instructor costs = 375 ducats	Instructor costs = 375 ducats
Room and other delivery costs = 100 ducats	Other administrative and delivery costs = 100 ducats
Travel costs = 400 ducats (for students and instructor)	Travel costs = 0 (for students and instructor)
Total cost "old way" = 1,000 ducats.	Total cost with e-learning = 900 ducats. You save 100 ducats.[1]

1. Of course, to put this in real business terms, you have to figure the dates when the costs are incurred, the dates when the benefits are realized, and adjust everything for the present value of money so that you are comparing apples to apples. This is important to do in real life, and I expect you know all about that from other ROI analyses you've already done in other parts of your business.

Let's step through the numbers here so you understand what's going on:

1. The courseware costs increase because for the classroom training you would do a minor update to existing material you've used before. But the courseware for the e-learning approach needs significantly more work to get it into a form that can be delivered over the Internet. (While you can teach the same "material" in the classroom and by e-learning, you need to do work to put that material into an e-learning form.) After the first conversion, you'll get back to doing updates just like you did for classroom courses—so this cost will fall over time.

2. The communications costs (to tell prospective students that the course is available) exist for both cases, but the higher cost for the e-learning case reflects the situation that you need to communicate more about the new style of learning as well.

3. The instructor costs are roughly the same whether it's classroom or e-learning delivery.

4. For the classroom, you need a room, and there will be other costs like printed student materials. For e-learning, there will be costs for administering the e-learning system that manages the delivery of such e-learning courses.

There is an old story about how computer technology made the impossible possible. Imagine you're running an insurance company in the 1950s and you are handling claims by hand. You have a small army of clerks and buildings full of filing cabinets. Lots and lots of filing cabinets. You are considering buying one of the new mainframe computers to automate the claims processing. You will be tempted to make the computer purchase decision on the basis of cost savings. That would make sense for what you know, but what you don't know is that on the business horizon are new U.S. government health programs. But you will not be able to bid for those huge government contracts with manual claims processing—it's just too slow, no matter how may clerks and filing cabinets you have. (In the same way, the U.S. Government Census Bureau moved to automated tabulating machines around 1900 because they were still counting the last population census by hand when it was time to take the next census.) Without the new mainframe computer, you can't get in the game of processing government health claim forms.

5. For the classroom course, students and instructors need to travel to the class. For the e-learning course, they don't travel.

Value-Focused ROI

E-learning enables improved value by letting you accomplish things that cannot be realized in other ways. This is a lot like what much of today's technology enables better, faster, cheaper.

Take this as an example: A high-tech company needs to provide regular product update training for its salespeople, who are spread about in many geographic locations (see Case Study #1 in Chapter 2). With e-learning, you can quickly train all the salespeople on everything they need to know about selling the new product. Without e-learning, it will take so long to roll out a new product sales course to all the salespeople that you won't even try. You'd have to be satisfied with an incompletely trained sales force—and that's going to mean you're losing revenue because of missed opportunities and basic sales mistakes that could have been corrected with a little training

Here's the general shape of a value-focused ROI analysis:

Potential Benefit	Cost of E-Learning Solution
You'll gain an additional 1,000 ducats in revenue if you can get all your salespeople quickly up to speed on selling the new product. If you can't get those salespeople up to speed quickly, then you don't achieve the 1,000 ducats.	❏ Courseware costs = 100 ducats ❏ Delivery costs = 100 ducats ❏ Communications costs = 50 ducats ❏ Instructor costs = 200 ducats ❏ Travel costs = 0
Total benefit = 1,000 ducats	Total cost = 450 ducats

Your total gain is the total benefit (1,000) minus the total cost (450), or 550 ducats.

Let's step through the table so you understand what's going on. First of all, your projected revenue is 1,000 ducats. Then your costs break down like this:

1. Courseware costs: You need to develop the courseware to be delivered in an e-learning form.

2. Delivery costs: There will be some costs to deliver the courseware from an e-learning system.

3. Communication costs: You will need to promote the course to your target students.

4. Instructor costs: This is the time that the instructor takes to prepare for and teach the course.

5. There are no travel costs for either the students or the instructor.

So, if you subtract your costs (450) from your revenue (1,000), you get your gain of 550 ducats.

3-5. How much confidence should you put in an ROI?

❏ An ROI is a analysis tool. You use it as input for your business decisions.

❏ Think of an ROI as a speedometer on your car—it doesn't control how you drive but gives you one measurement that will influence how you drive.

Tell Me More

It's reassuring to look at the numbers and pick the answer based on what the numbers say. ("Case A says we gain 500 ducats, and case B says we gain only 450 ducats. Clearly we go with Case A.") It seems very objective. All the subjectivity seems to have been driven out.

But my experience in dealing with good businesspeople is that ROI calculations are a guide and a double check for making good business decisions—not the other way around.

I know this sounds backwards at first. But I observe that good businesspersons don't simply follow where the numbers lead, positively or negatively. They know that the numbers are important, but they also know that there is a certain amount of subjectivity in even the most objective-looking numbers. Even if the ROI analysis says that you'll get one hundred ducats for every ducat you invest, that's a prediction, not a guarantee. Surprises can happen along the way to getting those one hundred ducats—predicted things might not occur, or unpredicted things might occur (war could break out, the stock market could crash, your key designer could be hit by a truck). An ROI analysis is a statement of what's likely to happen, at a reasonable risk level. The risk cannot be eliminated completely. It might not work out the way the numbers seem to promise.

Besides the fact that predictions of the future don't always work, ROI analyses are sometimes suspect because of the assumptions that went into calculating the numbers. Sometimes you'll find that the expected profit of a million ducats is built on faulty assumptions that will in fact result in a profit of only a hundred ducats. Or you might find that faulty assumptions cause you to turn down a good business alternative that the ROI understates.

There are lots of pitfalls—but if you're a successful businessperson, then you already know about these pitfalls. And you already know that making good business decisions is like making good bets at the race track. It's important to do your homework and at least check the racing form. It's even better, however, if you do your homework and also have a knack for picking winners.

3-6. What are your make/buy elements for e-learning?

❑ There are several e-learning elements that you can decide to make or buy:
  ❑ Courseware
  ❑ Instructors
  ❑ Learning management system (LMS)
  ❑ Hosting

Tell Me More

As in many other areas of your business, one of the big decisions you make about e-learning will be whether to build your own (make) or get it from someone else (buy). Alternately, you can also build some of the solution and buy other portions of the solution ready-made. How you handle this make/buy decision will affect your costs.

You can certainly make everything yourself for your e-learning system. Or you can buy some or all of the parts as indicated below:

E-Learning	Make/Buy Option
Courseware	There is a great deal of "off the shelf" courseware that you can license for your employees. You probably don't always have to create a course on learning to use MS Word because someone else has already developed that and will be very willing to license it to you.
	Or, you can send your employees to any number of existing Learning Portals on the Internet to get training on "standard" topics.
Learning management system (LMS)	In brief, an LMS handles the administration and delivery of e-learning courses.
	❑ You can buy your own LMS and set it up within your company.
	❑ Or, you can use one of the application service providers (ASPs) to set up a view into one of their existing LMSs on the Internet.

E-Learning	Make/Buy Option
Instructors	If you use instructor-led e-learning courses, you have the choice of using your own employees as instructors (make) or getting contract instructors to do the job (buy).
Hosting (where your e-learning system resides)	You can put your e-learning system within your own company, or you can use public e-learning sites, or you can use an ASP. (See Chapter 10 for a full description of these alternatives.)

3-7. What do e-learning "solution providers" cost?

❑ Costs for an e-learning solution provider will vary depending on the complexity of your problem and the quality you demand in the final solution.

❑ It also depends on when you're reading this book since costs of almost everything dealing with computers tend to fall over time.

❑ This is not much different than asking what it will cost to roof your house. Answer: "It depends."

Tell Me More

If you don't build all the parts of your e-learning system, then you are going to buy some or all of it from e-learning solution providers (sometimes called "vendors"). For example, IBM's Mindspan organization is an e-learning solution provider that develops e-learning courseware, sells the Lotus LearningSpace product (an LMS), and constructs complete e-learning solutions for e-learning clients. IBM Mindspan has a number of competitors in the industry—you have a wide range of vendor choices.

Dealing with e-learning solution providers is a lot like dealing with anyone else selling you a product or service.

1. You figure out what you need.
2. You ask one or more solution providers what they would charge to provide it.

So what will it cost you? That's a reasonable question. But of course, I can't give you an exact price since so much depends on what you're really asking for. Plus it depends on when you're reading this book. Costs of things in the computer industry tend to fluctuate a lot as they trend down over time. By the time you read any price I'd quote, it would have changed several times already.

After you talk to a couple of potential solution providers, however, you'll have a good idea of what the current costs are. In the same way, once you talk to a couple of roofing contractors you know that the costs will range from $1,500 to $3,500—and will depend on the type of shingles you choose and the quality of workmanship that the roofing contractor promises.

Chapter Summary

❑ The costs for e-learning can range widely, just as the costs of buying a car range widely.

❑ You could spend hundreds, or you could spend multi-millions.

❑ The cost components for e-learning include the courseware, the course delivery expenses (including instructors), marketing/promotional communications with the students, and administration and support expenses.

❑ The biggest thing influencing your e-learning costs is the size and complexity of your training problem.

❑ There are only a handful of other factors that account for the dimensions of a training problem.

❑ You can't avoid risk. But doing a return on investment (ROI) analysis lets you quantify the risk.

❑ There are two types of ROI analysis you can do for e-learning:
  ❑ Cost analysis: How it saves money (if you already have existing training you're spending on).
  ❑ Value analysis: How it improves value (lets you do things you couldn't do before).

❑ An ROI is an analysis tool. You use it as input to your business decisions.

❑ Think of an ROI as a speedometer on your car—it doesn't control how you drive but gives you one measurement that will influence how you drive.

❑ Costs for an e-learning solution provider will vary depending on the complexity of your problem and the quality you demand in the final solution.

❑ It also depends on when you're reading this book since costs of almost everything dealing with computers tends to fall over time.

❑ This is not much different than asking what it will cost to roof your house. Answer: "It depends."

CHAPTER FOUR

Applying E-Learning to Your Business

AJAX: "I will go learn more of it."

—William Shakespeare's *Troilus and Cressida*

As a businessperson, you shouldn't be surprised if applying e-learning to a business has many of the same characteristics as applying a new financial system or implementing a new HR benefits package for your employees. It will cost time and money to get it up and running, but if you plan with care and roll it out in a thoughtful manner, it will probably give you the benefits you projected.

Questions and Answers in This Chapter

4-1.   What is an e-learning success for you?

4-2.   What are typical barriers for implementing e-learning in a company?

4-3.   What does e-learning need from your management team?

4-4.   How critical is leading-edge technology to e-learning?

4-5.   Do you need to scrap your classroom training?

4-6.   How will your employees respond to e-learning?

4-7.   How does student motivation affect e-learning?

4-8.   How will instructors respond to e-learning?

4-9.   What global considerations do you need to
            take into account for e-learning?

4-1. What is an e-learning success for you?

❏ An e-learning success has to be in business terms, not in
    training terms. The entire reason you're involved with
    training is for business improvement.

Tell Me More

Some people think an e-learning success is lots of people attending
the class. Others think that a success is getting students to learn a
lot of stuff.

In fact, if you're a businessperson, an e-learning success is
something that makes a positive business impact. The bottom line
is that you're a businessperson, and you're investing in e-learning
to help your business, not as part of a public service program. And
it's important that you be as clear as you can about your success
criteria. For when you're caught up in the heat of day-to-day work,
it's very easy to lose sight of what you're trying to accomplish.

To make this specific, let's look at possible success objectives
for the case studies from Chapter 2:

E-Learning Case Study	Purpose	Success Objective
Note: These case studies are described in detail in Chapter 2.		
1. Product sales update training	Train salespeople in many countries around the world on your new product so they can start selling right away.	All the salespeople are trained well enough on the product to start selling it right away.

E-Learning Case Study	Purpose	Success Objective
2. *Technical certification training*	Provide ongoing training for hundreds of company engineers so they maintain their technical certification.	Each new engineer gets his certification within the allotted time. And each experienced engineer maintains his certification.
3. *Professional competency training*	Train hundreds of employees on company-defined skills competencies such as project management, consulting, IT system administration.	An agreed-on number of employees attain the target skill levels within a certain period of time. *Note: The objective here is not simply to provide training, but to make sure skill levels are being attained.*
4. *Business tools training*	Train hundreds of employees on new business tools that they are required to use on their jobs.	All employees needing to use the tool are trained to the required skill level.
5. *Technical skills training*	Train hundreds of employees on-demand for technical skills like Java programming, data mining, databases, and so on.	Employees can get the training they feel is needed to do their jobs. *Note: The objective here will be hard to measure.*
6. *"Ongoing professional" training*	Provide on-demand training for hundreds of employees in such professional skills as negotiating, running meetings, coaching, team dynamics, and so on.	Employees can get the training they feel is needed to do their jobs. *Note: The objective here will be hard to measure.*

E-Learning Case Study	Purpose	Success Objective
7. *New sales-person training in "how to sell"*	Train dozens of brand new sales-people each year—these new salespeople have never been in a sales job before.	Each new salesperson has the "basic skills" to enable the salesperson to start selling to customers.
8. *New-hire training*	Train dozens of new employees each year on what they need to know to be productive, contributing parts of your company.	New hires start to be productive, contributing members of your company. *Note: The objective here will be hard to measure.*
9. *New HR benefits training*	Train your entire employee popula-tion, around the world, on a new health-benefit plan for your company.	Employees feel they have enough knowledge of the HR benefits to make an informed choice. *Note: The objective here will be hard to measure.*
10. *Informal Technical Seminars*	Communicate leading-edge research via informal seminars.	New research is being communicated to the right people. *Note: The objective here will be hard to measure.*
11. *Legal compliance training*	Train hundreds of employees at several locations on government regulations and laws on such topics as sexual harass-ment, workplace diversity, and so on.	All employees know the regulations and laws at the required level.

Take special care when you have learning situations like #5, 6, 8, 9, and 10 in the preceding table. Getting good measurements of how those kinds of examples are really affecting your business will be hard to do. Now, don't get me wrong. I'm not suggesting that you avoid those kinds of learning situations. I'm only saying that you won't really be able to tell with a lot of confidence how effective you are being in those cases.

4-2. What are typical barriers for implementing e-learning in a company?

❑ If you have any experience at all with implementing and rolling out new things in a company, you know that there are always barriers and that it's best to know about them up front.

❑ Barriers to e-learning range from people's natural resistance to any kind of change, to new technology, to budget constraints.

Tell Me More

You'd like to think that there won't be any barriers. But if you have any experience at all in implementing something new and then rolling it out in a company, you know that there are always barriers. And it's better to know about them up front.

Barriers to moving to e-learning can include the following:

❑ *Natural resistance to change.* Students, training instructors, and managers are people, and people are creatures of habit. A rule of thumb is that people don't like change. So there's going to be resistance whenever you change old habits and procedures. As an example: Students who view traveling to class as a perk or as a vacation from work could be annoyed that the perk seems to have been taken away.

❑ *New instructor skills.* Training instructors will need to learn new ways of teaching at a distance. The old skills that work in the classroom don't always work with e-learning. And there are many things that are just plain different—like communicating with text instead of with a glance.

❑ *New technology.* Much of the technology for e-learning is very new. As a rule, new technology is more prone to problems than something that's been honed by years of experience. Furthermore, the e-learning standards are still pretty much under development, so sometimes you'll be surprised when one part of your e-learning system from one vendor just doesn't work with another part from another vendor.

❑ *Bandwidth limitations.* Most people still connect to the Internet at slow speeds. Plus, the Internet itself sometimes gets clogged. This is not a big deal for e-mail or for downloading most Web pages. But it can be a big deal for streaming video or audio.

❑ *Course availability.* Sometimes the course you want is available "off the shelf" and sometimes it's not. You might have to create your own e-learning courses, and that will take a little more thought and investment than getting a subject-matter expert in front of a room to show a few slides and do a chalk talk.

❑ *Budgets.* In many companies, training budgets are set years in advance, and the funding is allocated for traditional training. However, as you move to e-learning, you'll find that there are new costs (or at least costs that go into different accounting buckets). You might find that you're funding a different part of the IT organization than you ever worked with before.

4-3. What does e-learning need from your management team?

❑ Employees take their cues from management.
❑ Managers will need to keep realistic expectations, provide leadership, provide support, and manage the change that e-learning will bring to your company.

Tell Me More

Your company's management needs to give e-learning what it gives everything else: leadership and support. The success of e-learning in your company rests on the management team, just like the success of everything else in your business

Here's a quick list of what's needed from your management team:

1. *Realistic expectations.* Keep expectations at a reasonable level. Just because the learning is now being delivered over the Internet doesn't mean that the learning problem is "solved." Learning will still take time and effort by each individual student.

2. *Leadership.* Managers should be leading the way with e-learning. What's not useful is half-hearted communication based on an incomplete understanding of what's going on. Perhaps the most important thing your management team can do is fully understand what your e-learning initiative really does. And the best way to do that is to take a few e-learning courses and see what it feels like. (I don't mean just look at a five-minute demo, but actually take some of the courses.)

3. *Support.* Experience shows that some managers will think that e-learning enables students to take courses in no time at all since the students aren't going off to class. Furthermore, some e-learners will need management encouragement to keep up their motivation in relative isolation instead of being swept along with the pace of a face-to-face class.

4. *Willingness to manage change.* Depending on how much training your company does, e-learning has the potential to make a significant change to your company's culture. As a general rule, however, most people don't like to change. If you don't manage change, it can spin out of control. This is the same as anything you change in your business.

4-4. How critical is leading-edge technology to e-learning?

❑ Using leading-edge technology is important but not critical.

❑ The bottom line is the soundness of the instructional design. Students can learn from a simple presentation if it's instructionally sound. Students don't learn from a jazzy-looking multimedia experience if it's NOT instructionally sound.

Tell Me More

Using leading-edge technology is important but not critical. Sometimes it's only eye candy. Let me put it this way: Some of today's movies have spectacular special effects. But the best movies are not always the ones that use the most special effects. A good film is built first and foremost on the story. If the special effects support the story, then they can magnify the quality of a film. But if the special effects work against the story, or if they are just added on as extras, they will reduce the quality of the film. In the same way that it's the story for film, it's the instructional design for e-learning that is important.

With a strong instruction design, you can make an e-mail-based correspondence course work effectively (I know this for a fact because I've done it.) With a weak instructional design, you will be hard-pressed to make the jazziest virtual classroom work effectively.

Furthermore, in e-learning and in everything else, fancier things usually cost more than simple things. Yet, sometimes you do in fact need the fancier thing. In Chapters 6 and 7, you'll see that there are a number of different styles and building blocks for e-learning. Some of them are plain and simple. And some of them are pretty fancy technologically. But just because it's fancier doesn't always mean it'll get you better instructional impact.

Let me say it again. The bottom line is the soundness of the instructional design.

- ❑ Students can learn from a simple presentation if it's instructionally sound.
- ❑ Students don't learn from a jazzy-looking multimedia event if it's NOT instructionally sound.

4-5. Do you need to scrap your classroom training?

- ❑ No. Use what you have in the short term.

❑ You can blend together classroom and e-learning in the medium term, and move exclusively to an e-learning approach in the long term.

Tell Me More

Classroom learning does not conflict with e-learning. They are really complementary approaches. One is not a bad approach with the other being a good approach.

If you have a lot of classroom courses, keep them. You don't need to revamp all your courses. Keep delivering classroom courses as long as they make business sense for you.

In other words, use up what you have. When your inventory is depleted, you can move to the new e-learning format.

4-6. How will your employees respond to e-learning?

❑ E-learning will be a "different experience" for many of your employees. It will feel different. Some people enjoy trying things that feel different. Others don't.

❑ You will have to deal with e-learning challenges such as unfamiliarity, lack of self-motivation, lack of time, and the perception that it's contrary to company culture.

Tell Me More

Perhaps the most important thing to realize about e-learning is that *it feels different to the student* from traditional face-to-face learning experiences.

I think you'll best conceptualize the e-learning challenges if you think in terms of the differences between holding a face-to-face meeting in a conference room and holding a meeting where everyone is connected by telephone. The problems are similar—because people act different when they are face-to-face and when they aren't.

Many students thrive in an e-learning environment, but not all of them do. Student challenges include the following:

❑ *Unfamiliarity.* E-learning is new to many employees, and some will find it hard to adjust to the new learning situation. We sometimes forget how long it takes to get familiar with any new technology. Look at the blinking 12:00 on the VCR display in many people's homes to understand how widespread even small technology barriers really can be.

❑ *Lack of self-motivation.* Students only get out of education what they put into it. Remember that with e-learning, students must take more responsibility for learning the material. Not everyone is able to do that. Some people find it hard to stay motivated while they're learning away from a classroom. Also, the rule of thumb is that even the most highly motivated e-learning student starts to lose interest after about two weeks of calendar time, regardless of how many hours a day the class meets.

❑ *Lack of time.* Some students learn faster or slower than others. E-learning in a self-paced form can let students learn at their own pace. Training can be spread out over a period of days or weeks, a little bit each day. But all students need time to spend on the learning sessions, even if they are at their desk at work; they can't do the learning tasks and still do their regular work at the same time. Or, in some companies, employees might be expected to do their e-learning at home, before work, or after work instead of on work time.

❑ *Feelings of isolation.* The students can feel isolated. The familiar physical environment of the classroom, including the immediate presence of the teacher and other students, is missing. The environment is ingrained in some people as part of the way they learn—and some people will find it hard to learn in a different environment. (Like falling asleep on your back after years of falling asleep on your stomach.)

❑ *Feelings of going against company culture.* "Let me interrupt you for just a few minutes about an urgent work problem" says the manager while the employee is trying to take an e-learning course at her desk. Other employees tell you that if the training were really important, they'd send you away to class.

What this comes down to is that you have to go to extra lengths to support the students taking e-learning courses if you want your e-learning program to be a success. Can you help motivate and encourage them in positive ways? Can you help remove distractions and help make sure they have the time to do the e-learning coursework?

4-7. How does student motivation affect e-learning?

❑ Learning is work, not entertainment.
❑ E-learning is even more work than learning in a classroom environment.
❑ Many people are accustomed to learning only in the traditional classroom environment and find it hard to learn "on their own."

Tell Me More

Except for the fortunate few, learning is work, not fun. This means that, at the very least, you need to put training into a different problem frame from entertainment. Put it this way: How many people do you see reading John Grisham novels? Now how many do see reading *Teach Yourself Java in 24 Hours* or *How to Think About Statistics?*

Learning takes effort and concentration, and most students can't learn by just putting their brains on automatic the way they can when they watch television. Take a straw poll sometime and see for yourself: How many of your associates would rather learn something new or watch TV? We believe that it's an axiom of human nature that "Left to themselves, most people will turn to entertainment and not to making the effort to learning something new."

Learning also takes time. Most students can't just glance at something once and have it stick in their long-term memory. And if you're talking about building skills, it's even more time-consuming. There's a reason that professional basketball players practice shooting every day. It's the same reason professional musicians spend hours at practice every day. Real skills are hard to develop and hard to maintain.

I tell people to think of learning the way they would think of cooking an omelet. You can't hurry an omelet—unless you want a bad omelet. Let me put it another way—learning is not the same kind of thing as pouring water from a pitcher into a cup.

Given that learning is hard, time-consuming work, what would motivate a student to go through the pain? Some key student motivations include:

- ❑ The course teaches something that is critical to doing the immediate job.
- ❑ The student is working toward a certification or a degree.
- ❑ The student is required by management to prove that they completed such and such a course.

The following table identifies some of the student motivations for the case studies from Chapter 2:

E-Learning Case Study *Note: These case studies are described in detail in Chapter 2.*	Purpose	Student Motivation
1. *Product sales update training*	Train salespeople in many countries around the world on your new product so they can start selling right away.	Critical to doing immediate job. Students know that management insists that they get this training right now and will be taking roll.
2. *Technical certification training*	Provide ongoing training for hundreds of company engineers so they maintain their technical certification.	Critical to doing immediate job. Students know that management insists that they get this training right now and will be taking roll.

E-Learning Case Study	Purpose	Student Motivation
3. *Professional competency training*	Train hundreds of employees on company-defined skills competencies such as project management, consulting, IT system administration.	Important to job, but not immediate. Students can "put it off" if they think they have higher priority things to do.
4. *Business tools training*	Train hundreds of employees on new business tools that they are required to use on their jobs.	Critical to doing immediate job. Students know that management insists that they get this training right now and will be taking roll.
5. *Technical skills training*	Train hundreds of employees on-demand for technical skills like Java programming, data mining, databases, and so on.	Students who have a strong job need to learn a particular topic will be highly motivated. Students with a weaker job need can "put it off" if they think they have higher priority things to do.
6. *"Ongoing professional" training*	Provide on-demand training to hundreds of employees in such professional skills as negotiating, running meetings, coaching, and team dynamics.	Important to students in a general sense. Students can "put it off" if they think they have higher priority things to do.

E-Learning Case Study	Purpose	Student Motivation
7. *New salesperson training in "how to sell"*	Train dozens of brand new salespeople each year—these new sales people have never been in a sales job before.	Critical to doing immediate job. Students know failure to demonstrate the attainment of sales skills will impact their ability to continue doing their job.
8. *New-hire training*	Train dozens of new employees each year on what they need to know to be productive, contributing parts of your company.	New hires will be strongly motivated until they think they have learned enough to be productive employees, then the interest will tail off.
9. *New HR benefits training*	Train your entire employee population, around the world, on a new health-benefit plan for your company.	Employees will be motivated to the extent they think they have a knowledge gap. If they think they already know enough about the new benefits, they will not be interested in training about it.
10. *Informal technical seminars*	Communicate leading-edge research via informal seminars	Researchers will be highly interested in topics that touch on their areas of research. Otherwise, they will have very little interest.

E-Learning Case Study	Purpose	Student Motivation
11. *Legal compliance training*	Train hundreds of employees at several locations on government regulations and laws on such topics as sexual harassment, workplace diversity, and so on.	Critical to doing immediate job. Students know that management insists that they get this training right now and will be taking roll.

4-8. How will instructors respond to e-learning?

❑ Teaching an e-learning course is, in fact, harder than teaching a classroom course.

❑ Instructors who have honed their skills toward the classroom experience will need to learn new "how to teach in an e-learning environment" skills.

Tell Me More

Teaching in an e-learning environment isn't easier—it's harder. For example, one challenge for an instructor in the classroom is to notice when a student is confused or falling behind. Instructors need to know how to do the same thing when running an e-learning class, and the fact is, it's not easy. Many experienced instructors might have been teaching successfully for years in the classroom, but they still have very little experience with teaching by means of e-learning.

Let's look at two typical examples of e-learning instruction:

Example 1: Synchronous E-Learning

With synchronous e-learning, the instructor and all the students meet at the same time and are connected by technology that acts like real-time interactive audio and video. The instructor and all the students can interact at least by voice, and the instructor's "chalk talking" can be communicated to the student as the instructor draws.

As instructors try this type of teaching, they find that one-way communicating, from the instructor to the student (lecture) can occur quite easily. However, answering questions by the students takes quite a bit longer than answering questions in a face-to-face classroom. And it's hard for the instructor to really tell if the whole class is following along, or if some of the students have fallen asleep, gone out for coffee, or are surfing the Web in another computer window.

Example 2: Asynchronous Collaboration

With asynchronous collaboration, instructors and students don't meet at exactly the same time. Instead, the instructor will post assignments in a team room, students will be expected to complete the assignments within a short period of time, and the instructor and students interact by exchanging messages that are posted to a bulletin board or team room. In this case, answering questions from the student can take hours or days, and the instructor has a very hard time keeping her finger on the pulse of the class. It's very difficult to tell which students are getting it and which are getting lost.

From these examples, we can see that the instructor will face some significant challenges, summarized in the following table.

Challenge	Consideration
New tools for teaching	Instructors no longer have a traditional, familiar classroom. Instead they are communicating via e-mail, via team rooms and bulletin boards, via recorded voice. They need to adapt a teaching style that works in the classroom so that it works remotely.
	Instructors need to understand and be adept at the delivery technology without being distracted from their teaching role. They'll get questions about the course but

Challenge	Consideration

	also questions from students who can't get the technology to work right for them—the instructor turns into part help-desk.
Time	Almost everything about teaching at a distance takes longer. Just opening all the student e-mail takes time. Giving thoughtful replies takes even more time: Most people can talk faster than they can type.
Student interaction	It's hard to tell whether e-learning students are really "getting it." In the traditional classroom, instructors have many techniques for telling if the class is really following along with them. Just figuring out the needs of distant students without face-to-face contact is very hard at first.
	Face-to-face feedback (e.g., students' questions, comments, body language, and facial expressions) is lacking until interactive video is a real possibility.
	Finding convenient opportunities to talk to students individually is difficult. (Going for coffee together after class is no longer an option.)

4-9. What global considerations do you need to take into account for e-learning?

- ❑ If your e-learning will have a global reach, you need to think long and hard about:
    - ❑ Language
    - ❑ Time zones
    - ❑ Cultural differences (learning styles, humor)

Tell Me More

If your company is a global business, then you already know that communication within a global company is significantly different from communication within a company that operates within a single country. The global considerations are a result of these communication factors:

1. *Language.* You will have to solve the language problem. Students from different countries and different cultures will speak different languages. There are two main approaches to this, neither of which is perfect:

   ❏ Make different versions of the e-learning courseware in different languages. You can immediately see the cost of doing it this way.

   ❏ Insist that all students around the world speak a common language. You'll have to pick a single language and figure out what to do with students who can't speak it.

2. *Time zones.* When it's 8 A.M. in New York City, it's 9 P.M. in Tokyo. This is a significant problem if you need to have students and instructors communicating at the same time during the class. The solution, of course, is to emphasize more asynchronous communications: bulletin board messages, team room messages/responses, etc.

3. *Culture.* Different cultures have different rules for what is appropriate, for what is funny, for what is embarrassing, for what is obscene. Different cultures also have different predominant learning styles: Asking questions might be appropriate in one culture and inappropriate in another. Running multicultural classes, which e-learning enables, is a challenge for the instructional design, for the human instructor, and for the students in the class.

Chapter Summary

❏ An e-learning success has to be thought of in business terms, not in training terms. The entire reason you're involved with training is for business improvement.

❑ If you have any experience at all with implementing and rolling out new things in a company, you know that there are always barriers and that it's best to know about them up front.

❑ Barriers to e-learning range from people's natural resistance to any kind of change, to new technology, to budget constraints.

❑ Employees take their cues from management, and managers will be expected to keep realistic expectations, provide leadership, provide support, and manage the change that e-learning will bring to your company.

❑ Using leading-edge technology is important but not critical.

❑ The bottom line is the soundness of the instructional design. Students can learn from a simple presentation if it's instructionally sound. Students don't learn from a jazzy-looking multimedia event if it's NOT instructionally sound.

❑ E-learning will be a "different experience" for many of your employees. It will feel different. Some people enjoy trying things that feel different. Others don't.

❑ You will have to deal with e-learning challenges such as unfamiliarity, lack of self-motivation, lack of time, and the perception that it's contrary to company culture.

❑ Learning is work, not entertainment.

❑ Many people are accustomed to learning only in the traditional classroom environment and find it hard to learn "on their own."

❑ Teaching an e-learning course is, in fact, harder than teaching a classroom course.

❑ Instructors who have honed their skills toward the classroom experience will need to learn new skills.

❑ If your e-learning will have a global reach, then you need to think long and hard about:
  ❑ Language
  ❑ Time zones
  ❑ Cultural differences (learning styles, humor)

CHAPTER FIVE

What Do Today's E-Learning Thought Leaders Say?

PRINCE HAL: " . . . for wisdom cries out in the street and no man regards it."

—William Shakespeare's *Henry IV*

You're about half way through the book, and now is a good time for a change of pace.

I interviewed several of the leading thought leaders in the e-learning field, and this chapter is the result of those interviews. Each of these thought leaders is on the job every day working to make e-learning a reality in companies around the world.

All of these thought leaders are forward thinkers, but more importantly, they each have strong practical experience. They know today's state of the art and what's really practical to do, both today and into the near future. And they each know that making e-learning a success for a company is more than a question of technology—it's also a question of company culture, project focus, and leadership.

Thought Leader Interviews in This Chapter

5-1. Elliott Masie

Elliott Masie is an internationally recognized speaker, futurist, humorist, author, and consultant on the critical topics of technology, business, learning and workplace productivity. Elliott is the editor of *TechLearn Trends*, an internet newsletter read by over 41,000 business executives worldwide, and the editor of *Learning Decisions*, a subscription newsletter. He heads The MASIE Center (www.masie.com), a thinktank focused on how organizations can absorb technology and create continuous learning and knowledge within the workforce. Elliott's professional focus has been to demystify the world of technology in order to allow organizations to use their wisdom and resources to make key choices.

Question: What do you see as the impact of e-learning on companies and enterprises?

Elliott Masie: I think there are two things. The most important thing is that it greatly expands the perception of the reach of learning and training and knowledge interventions without being limited by the overhead cost of "When can we do it by?", "Can we get people there?", "Can we get an instructor there?", and "Do we have a facility?"

So one of the impacts is that it's applying the same kind of empowerment that other kinds of "e-processes" do. I think it's profound that there are fewer conversations now about "I wish I could train a lot of people, but I can't, so I'll only train a few." There's more of a sense of "OK, if I need them to be trained, I'll reach them with an appropriate way to do it."

The second impact, from a business point of view, is that there is a growing excitement about leveraging learning as a strategic tool—both from a talent deployment point of view and ultimately from a point of view of using it for extending and enriching the customer relationship with knowledge, learning, and training.

Question: Do you think the impact is something to look for now, or is it still in the future?

Elliott Masie: When you think of the empowerment perspective I just spoke about, then people perceive that right now. I think, given the sophistication and the levels of investment we're seeing in some organizations, there are lines of business that are achieving it right now. Certainly with the IT business units today, there is less of a perception that "I have to wait to send them to class." They'll say "What does Netg, or SmartForce, or IBM have as resources?" so they can start to learn today.

We're doing a major rewrite of an application in my own firm, and my statement to my group was "What do you need to learn?" and their first reaction was "Let me see what's online." Five years ago it would have been "Let me call the training company nearby and see when their next class is."

So I think depending on the infrastructure and on the readiness, business units are doing this today. I think we're seeing a pretty steady slope rise in that, and there are early arrivers and mid-arrivers, and early followers and late followers.

Question: Can you tell us about a specific company where you know e-learning has been implemented?

Elliott Masie: I'll give you two, one a government example and one a corporate example.

The government example is the U.S. Department of Defense. The current military situation in Afghanistan is a perfect example of how intensive e-learning is taking place. You can't train somebody for a vague mission. What we're seeing is that people get trained to a certain level, and the final training takes place on the plane, in the tent in the field, at the base, and sometimes even through a handheld device. The military is a walking example of the sense of learning empowerment that is being felt.

A year and a half ago, I toured a submarine with the U.S. Secretary of Defense, and the captain of the submarine said that the schedule there is that the sailors are on duty for ten hours, they sleep for a couple of hours, and they eat for an hour. And then they don't have anything to do. In the old days they watched video games, but now most of them are taking classes—whether it's training about equipment on board or classes for pursuing a community college degree back in Virginia. So I think they are really a walking example of this learning empowerment you get with e-learning.

Here's my corporate example, in the pharmaceutical sector. There are at least four organizations right now that have changed, or are changing, the footprint for the training of new-hire sales reps, and the footprint of new-product launch training, both of which were extremely cost-intensive, residentially-based boot camps, lasting from three to five weeks. The boot camps still happen, but they are a much smaller footprint and they are incredibly more scalable, both globally and regionally. The bulk of the knowledge transfer is happening through asynchronous and synchronous online and distributed events.

Question: With regard to e-learning, do you think the impact on medium- and small-size companies is different from that on large companies?

Elliott Masie: The small companies haven't really stepped up to it for the most part. Part of it is that the marketplace is not really understanding their needs. The average small company is less likely to be tracking this, and the only arena that they are likely to be doing e-learning in is IT training, and the odd soft-skill training.

I think medium-size companies are doing it even better than the really big companies, sometimes, I think, because the medium-size companies want to act like big companies in a lot of ways.

But I think the market still has to figure out what the small-size company needs.

Question: How should companies get started with e-learning?

Elliott Masie: I think there are three things they should do.

One of the things is to ask the question "What training have we never been able to do in classrooms?" Not "What's our most popular training?" But what's something we never got around to. Then look for some off-the-shelf e-learning content that they can buy from a third party and start to apply as an optional or required piece. Say "You've always wanted training on X, and here's a way to do that."

The second thing I would look at is the use of instructor-led virtual classroom experiences, because you can get to that quickly. You can get a tool from IBM or another vendor, and you get one of your subject-matter experts and you can start to provide e-learning that doesn't require a lot of authoring.

I think the third is going to take a little longer. And that's to look for something that's going to drive a little revenue or significantly cut back expenses. I am convinced that for driving revenue the way to go is to look at those things that speed time to market for selling, or will speed time to deploy for new hires. And I'd pick a small project with high revenue impact, something that is closely related to observable revenue gains or significant cost impacts. Now along the way they are going to need a strategy and an infrastructure, and all that good stuff, but this way will give them a proof of concept and get them buy-in pretty quickly.

Question: Are you aware of any well-known pitfalls that companies should watch out for as they get started with e-learning?

Elliott Masie: Absolutely. As much as I think that learning management systems are a part of the fabric, and that they are a necessary complexity (I won't say a necessary evil), it is important for organizations to really, really crawl and walk before they enter a marathon.

It's really important to go out and have the experiences without buying the infrastructure. Rent it, host it externally, borrow the tool, get them through a content provider. But it's really important to get an internal attitude about what works, what's important, what's valuable, and then go on from there.

Question: Have you taken e-learning courses yourself? What was your experience?

Elliott Masie: I think that e-learning works as well as the classroom works. I know that's a provocative statement. Remember though that there are good, bad, excellent, and inferior classroom experiences and in the same sense there is good, bad, excellent, and inferior e-learning

A cheap classroom course doesn't work, and cheap e-learning doesn't work either. A cheap class would be to put an uninteresting, unfocused, poorly prepared instructor in front of a thousand people, show a million slides, and don't allow questions from the learners. That doesn't work. And we've all been there. The digital equivalent of that is to pull together a hundred slides, make it uninteresting, and make it simply reading, and have the situation where there are no questions possible from the learners. So bad e-learning is going to fail as much as bad classroom training.

Now if I as the student want the outcome, if I'm motivated to get to the end of the training because it's a piece of information that lets me do my job better, if it's a skill that lets me leave my job and go to another job, it takes away pain, it lets me look good in front of my boss, whatever the student motivation is, if the course succeeds at that, to me it works. And e-learning works!

The mistake we make in some ways is to think we can dip learners into e-learning and it's going to work regardless of whether there is student motivation or whether there is good instructional design.

The biggest gains I see are when e-learning gets the mind of the learner going and turns them from a passive viewer into an active participant. And I really see some great ways that e-learning does that, through simulations, threaded discussions, and real-time conversations.

If it gets the mind going, if it creates an activity instead of being just a content viewer, then I think that e-learning can be very compelling. And I think that over time we'll get better at doing that. The early arriver, the cheap stuff where we took an instructor-led course or, worse yet, took a textbook, and just put it online to get a digital page-turner, doesn't work any more than having an instructor read to a class full of students from a book.

As we reveal and get a marketplace hunger for the really compelling stuff, I think the e-learning content will follow. There are not a lot of technology hurdles—of course, there are some bandwidth challenges and there are some firewall issues—but ultimately we'll just get better and better at streaming, personalizing, collaborating, and communicating, and all of those enabling functions that are technology-based. We'll harvest them all for better e-learning.

Question: If you were sharing a taxi to the airport with a CEO of a company who wanted your recommendations about e-learning, what would you tell that CEO?

Elliott Masie: If the CEO asked me whether to use e-learning in his company, I'd say two things.

First, I'd use the best mixture of what you're now doing (formal training, informal training, one-on-one job assisting, and books given out) and I'd add to look for the emerging power of e-learning, which would include online classes, asynchronous content, collaboration, learning communities. I would link it all to knowledge management and look to integrate it into your systems so that people don't have to leave work to learn, but learning becomes part of work.

The final thing I would say is to take a look at your kids (or if you're older, look at your grandkids). They are natural learners. To them the computer is not a place they go to program—very few of these kids program. It's not a computing device. It's a knowledge, communications, and collaboration device. It's a door that lets them get to what they need to know. And just as that executive's children are figuring this out, their parents and grandparents are figuring it out, too.

So this is happening now, but it will increasingly be part of the future. They have no choice. The only choice is whether to do it well.

5-2. Janis Morariu

Janis Morariu, Ph.D., is the Principal for Learning Strategy and Design at IBM Learning Services. Janis has over twenty years of experience in maximizing individual and organizational performance through training and performance support strategies and solutions for a wide variety of audiences and industries, ranging from healthcare professionals to international bankers, government agencies, nonprofit organizations, and kindergarten through college educational institutions. She received her doctorate in cognitive psychology from the University of Nebraska and an Ed.S. and M.S. in instructional systems technology from Indiana University. She has published over thirty articles and presented at over thirty-five conference sessions in the fields of technology-based training, distributed learning, electronic performance support systems (EPSS), and knowledge management.

Question: What do you see as the impact of e-learning on companies and enterprises?

Janis Morariu: I see the major impact of well-designed e-learning as being on performance and productivity, both for the individual and the organization as a whole. That's really what e-learning is targeting with the right performance-based strategies.

With e-learning, employees will be provided with greater training opportunities that can take them beyond just conceptual and procedural understanding. It can take them into decision-making and problem-solving, and that impacts productivity tremendously.

Question: Do you think the impact is something to look for now, or is it still in the future?

Janis Morariu: I see some of it happening now. But the greater impact is in the future. I don't see very good focus on measurements within corporations that can help quantify the return on investment and the real impact of e-learning on the company.

Most companies today are talking about the impact of e-learning in terms of cost avoidance, not having to send students to class, not having to pay for travel and hotels. Although that cost case is compelling, the real impact is going to come from showing measurable performance improvement and increased productivity.

Question: Do you hear companies asking for e-learning today, or do they consider it only after you suggest it?

Janis Morariu: Companies are definitely asking for e-learning today. They realize that they have to do things differently—some companies have dabbled in computer-based training, and others have had some very bad experiences in their past. When I talk to those companies, I am emphasizing all four tiers of learning—it's not just about moving the self-study computer-based training to the Web. It's really about leveraging technology so we can put people in touch with experts and each other to form powerful teams. In fact, what we're really aiming at is learning communities enabled through the technology.

Companies are asking us about our blended learning strategy because we are proving through our own global implementation and first-hand experience that it works, and that it can make a difference on the bottom line.

Question: Can you tell us about a specific company where you know e-learning has been implemented?

Janis Morariu: One airplane manufacturing company had a particularly hard time with their timeframes and their use of tools to meet production schedules. Our performance consultants were called in to improve the performance and productivity of the engineers. We streamlined processes, and improved the training approach. We showed a strong return on the training investment, with an emphasis on the productivity increases and dramatic reduction in errors and inefficiencies.

Another example is a pharmaceutical company that is using a customized version of the IBM e-learning-based management development curriculum. Their feedback to us is that this program is very well received and is providing a level of training and experience that they have not been able to provide in the past. It's about the flexibility of the e-learning, and the blending of different kinds of e-learning across the IBM 4-Tier Learning Model—from the online reference materials that people start with to the collaboration and teaming, saving the face-to-face training for those tasks and skills that really require it and can justify the cost of bringing people together.

I'm talking with a healthcare/insurance company right now that wants a very sophisticated system that integrates e-learning with knowledge management, with very strong collaborative community tools, so that they can more effectively leverage their "masters," or mentors, worldwide. This company is betting a lot of their business on using e-learning to get teams up to speed, to maintain teams and update skills, and to support these teams with "just-in-time" access to information, training, and experts. So the concept of just-in-time e-learning is very critical to the strategy of this company. Within a year, this company wants to establish e-learning collaboration technologies as an integral part of a much larger solution that includes ongoing workflow and performance support.

Question: How should companies get started with e-learning?

Janis Morariu: Companies that are getting started in the right way are making the investment in a very strong e-learning strategy. The e-learning strategy is not built around the technology, but around the business. Companies that lead with the strategy instead of the technology actually make better decisions with regard to the technology. They also consider the processes and resources that need to be in place to support the change in the way they'll be doing business. They are changing not only their training approaches and infrastructure, but their whole corporate culture and the way that people learn and work together.

I'm working with a large petroleum company right now who wants to convert all their instructor-led training to e-learning. They had a committee that was working on this for a number of months. My team is now helping them lay out in a scenario-based way what it really means to have people in their organization take e-learning courses, basic as well as more in-depth courses with a lot of teamwork and problem-solving going on. We've actually walked them through what it looks and feels like. They've recognized from this approach that they are going to have to change a lot about their corporate culture—it's not just about the technologies and infrastructure that they need to put in place.

They'll be supporting people in a whole different way from the time that they first come in the door to years later when they are experts in the company. Their strategy is built around accessibility and flexibility. We've gone through a number of scenarios about what that means, and we've redefined their e-learning strategy a few times before they've even made an investment in the technology and infrastructure to support it. They are actually better equipped to predict the impact on their organization by investing in a solid e-learning strategy *before* they invest in technology.

They are not only happy with this strategy-first approach, they've expressed relief that we are uncovering a number of things that they never even considered.

Question: Are you aware of any well-known pitfalls that companies should watch out for as they get started with e-learning?

Janis Morariu: Here's the biggest pitfall. What I've seen are a lot of companies putting out request for proposals (RFPs) for a learning management system (LMS). The focus is on the technology. These RFPs have a long list of requirements, which seem to be everything you'd ever want to consider in an LMS. They'll put these lists of requirements together, and you know that they don't have an e-learning strategy behind it just because of the requirements they list. We've responded to these RFPs, which typically result in a solution based on technologies and costs that are way beyond what these companies have budgeted. So, many of these companies have decided not to make the investment at this time.

Starting with the technology as the way to enter e-learning is absolutely the wrong way to do it.

Question: Have you taken e-learning courses yourself? What was your experience?

Janis Morariu: I've taken many different kinds of e-learning courses from going through Web reference material, to Web-based training, to live collaborative sessions.

One of the problems today is the connectivity, the size of the pipes when you're using rich media courses, and having to wait for things to load. I think this is why you have problems getting people to finish the self-paced Web courses they start. A big problem is how to keep people engaged, and one reason people disengage is the response time.

We also have to pay attention to the length of time that people are willing to spend to take Web-based training. It's different from the computer-based training we know from the past. For Web-based, I think twenty to thirty minutes is the right amount of seat time, and smaller modules are critical.

What I find is that there are a lot of Web-based training courses that just are not well-designed. It might be designed well for a CD-ROM delivery of computer-based training, but for the Web you really need a different eye. Usability design for the Web is different, and you really need to understand how people use the Web to design well for it.

When it's well-designed, it's fabulous. The problem is not enough experience with how to design and deliver for the Web. But I do see a trend with some very effectively designed Web-based training.

Question: If you were sharing a taxi to the airport with a CEO of a company who wanted your recommendations about e-learning, what would you tell that CEO?

Janis Morariu: If the CEO asks me whether her company should be using e-learning, I would say "absolutely." We have very strong evidence that it can impact the bottom line through increased productivity as well as cost avoidance. IBM itself has saved $350 million in cost avoidance, but the quality of the educational experience has increased and the level of training available has increased. This impacts people's performance and productivity.

Question: If you were to look ten years into the future, what do you think the e-learning situation will be like in companies?

Janis Morariu: I think we will have pervasive e-learning—it will be everywhere and you'll hardly even notice it. The technologies to enable pervasive e-learning will include such things as going through training modules on your handheld PDA, e-meetings and online just-in-time talks with an expert, and searching for best practices in our knowledge management tools. I see highly integrated, just-in-time training being built right into an employee's flow of work.

I think we'll still see instructor involvement, but the instructor will change. The instructor will be a master, or an expert, and it will be a virtual connection. The technology will give us a pervasive connection to the organization's masters and experts—much more than what we do today.

5-3. Steve Rae

Steve Rae, Worldwide Executive for IBM's Mindspan Services, specializes in applying proven business models to the world of e-learning, a perspective that helps clients implement successful distributed learning and knowledge management solutions. Steve has responsibility for a worldwide team of e-learning specialists and content-development resources deployed worldwide in over forty locations in twenty-three countries that span all the major geographies. He is responsible for the personnel that help deliver custom services for IBM's Mindspan Solutions, a premier provider of end-to-end e-learning solutions.

Question: What do you see as the impact of e-learning on companies and enterprises?

Steve Rae: I look at three impacts, and I'll start with the easiest one: cost avoidance. I believe that one of the profound impacts that e-learning has had on companies is to reduce the cost of training.

That's seen in a couple of ways. A company is able to reduce its training budget or its able to do more training with the same amount of money. IBM is a good use-case for this. If you look at our annual report last year, it says we saved over $350 million with e-learning, which takes into account all the content we have in e-learning and "What would it have cost us if we had delivered that in a traditional way?".

The second one is really about the ability to impact the performance of the organization. This one gets a little more difficult to measure and quantify, but e-learning enables us to provide environments in which we learn better (like collaborative and simulated environments), where we better prepare individuals for what they are supposed to do in the real workplace. That has an impact on the organization's ability to perform.

And the last one is a matter of speed. I hear companies talking about getting a product launch out to 30,000 people, and they need training as part of that. Again, IBM is a good example in what we did with the signature sales method (SSM). Our old method for getting everyone on board with SSM would have been to bring everyone in to two-day live workshops. Well if you look at how long that would have taken us versus our use of e-learning technology, you'll see that we compressed that tremendously.

So it's not only the ability to create better performance, but also the speed and time to performance. And to me, the last two are far more important than the straight cost avoidance I began with. Because cost avoidance doesn't take into account things like the opportunity cost associated with slow deployment of an initiative where you might get inconsistent messaging and inconsistent execution. What's most important is speed and performance, and especially "time to performance."

Question: Do you think the impact is something to look for now, or is it still in the future?

Steve Rae: I think the impacts are here today, and they are only going to get better. The things I talked about in the first question—cost avoidance, performance, and speed—are available to companies deploying these solutions today. But over time, here are some of the things I think are going to be better.

We'll see a better way to map an inventory of the skills of an organization to an aggregate training prescription that is then delivered on an individual basis. That is still something that is at a distance away from us today.

And as we go down the road, we will see much richer media. And I think we are still exploring the notion of what it means to provide structured informal learning, collaboration, and so forth, especially in an informal space. The richer media will make it better.

These things will only improve the value proposition that we have today.

Question: Can you tell us about a specific company where you know e-learning has been implemented?

Steve Rae: Let me first say what I think e-learning is really here to do. It's really here to amplify the human beings in the learning process, and not to displace them. In that vein, let me touch on a few things that I've seen companies do that are really interesting.

Think of the knowledge in a person on the shop floor who has the most in-depth knowledge of how a particular machine works. When that machine goes down, your entire center goes down. How do you get the knowledge of that individual to be spread among more individuals in a powerful and replicable way? So here's an example of a company that has taken such subject-matter experts from the shop floor, armed them with video cameras and some knowledge about how to structure learning content, and put them in the front end of the queue. These aren't professional instructional designers, but they have created content that can be delivered, and that has an impact on the learner. And the learner is really one of their peers.

What I'm saying is that this is a company that has figured out how to shorten the gap between the subject-matter expert and the learner, and that's what this is really all about. Everything that falls in between filters out learning. The more you put between the subject-matter expert and the learner filters the message.

Companies that are using live e-learning are another good example. I think of the companies that are using the live virtual classroom to provide training environments while their employees are on the road. It's a way to create the human connection.

And IBM itself has a large number of examples, from IBM management development to the way we've tied in knowledge networks, communities of practice, and all those things into a cohesive Web presence.

Question: With regard to e-learning, do you think the impact on medium- and small-size companies is different from that on large companies?

Steve Rae: I think there is a difference. The size of your learning audience has a lot to do with the benefit you will get from e-learning.

If you are a small company where everyone is collocated, you don't need to take all your learning content and put it into sophisticated technologies so you can deliver it to the guy next door.

My biggest concern when I look at big companies is their ability to get consistent execution. If they don't execute consistently, then they won't get the business impact that they envisioned from the initiative that got them involved with e-learning in the first place.

E-learning gives you the ability to deliver a more consistent message to a large audience, and larger companies have profoundly bigger value propositions to gain than small companies.

Question: How should companies get started with e-learning?

Steve Rae: The first thing, I think, is to put it in the context of a business initiative. They need to assess "Do I need e-learning?" Is there incremental value in using e-learning?

So if they are just getting started, that means that they have done this before with non-e-methods. Video tapes in the mail, traditional classes, those kinds of things. I think it is very important for them to identify exactly what is the incremental benefit they are looking for, very clearly establishing their goals of what they want to get out of e-learning.

E-learning has a very broad definition. It's everything from just creating reference Web pages, to building a certification program, to live virtual classroom spaces, to much more. Companies first need to clearly establish the objectives they want to achieve, and then look at how e-learning can best meet those. And because e-learning is such a broad landscape of capabilities, if they have no experience with it, my recommendation is to bring in some level of consulting.

The first few engagements can be really tough with e-learning. But I don't know how many major corporations are really left to get started. I believe that the collective experience of the marketplace is really at the point where everyone has some experience, and we can now do some interesting and innovative things.

Question: Are you aware of any well-known pitfalls that companies should watch out for as they get started with e-learning?

Steve Rae: The biggest pitfall is to define e-learning just as CBT (computer-based training). It's to assume this kind of experience: Go out, find a Web site, find a course, play the course, track student results. But I think that e-learning is really far more interesting than that.

I think that e-learning is about learning being pervasive. It's about using instant messaging to find an expert to answer a question right now. That's impact learning.

I think you have to look at e-learning as a much richer, pervasive presence in an organization that can make a profound impact. That thinking is embodied in the IBM 4-Tier Learning Model.

Question: Have you taken e-learning courses yourself? What was your experience?

Steve Rae: I've experienced many, many different kinds of e-learning.

I personally don't like the traditional CBT experience, although I think that's getting better too.

I really think the power of e-learning is in the live experience. There's something that's engaging about having a live, knowledgeable subject-matter expert—a human being. And some of the best e-learning experiences I've had have been at the hands of a very good e-facilitator.

The next thing that's just coming to the forefront is "immersive simulations." It's like the video games that I see my kids play where the game creates situations that they problem-solve around. The thing that fascinates me is that they may fail four or five times before they get it right, but once they get it right, they know it. The way that the learning has taken place, they know it with very high retention. I think the powerful learning environments will provide things like that, in contrast to "Here's some material, memorize it, because I'm going to ask you a test question on it." What I'm talking about is anything that is procedure-based, that has a flow to it with things you have to do. Like the sales process. This tests your ability to apply knowledge, not your ability to memorize information.

Question: If you were sharing a taxi to the airport with a CEO of a company who wanted your recommendations about e-learning, what would you tell that CEO?

Steve Rae: I would say to take an inventory of all the business initiatives that you have tried, and make an assessment of where the lack of a learning strategy had an impact on the failures, or the presence of a learning strategy had an impact on your successes.

Find the role that learning had to play, and look at how e-learning could make the successes better, and how e-learning could displace the failures.

Question: If you were to look ten years into the future, what do you think the e-learning situation will be like in companies?

Steve Rae: When I look down the road, I look for a huge amount of interoperable content. You're going to be able to tap into every publisher's content, and it's going to interoperate so you will be able to build learning sequences that are based on this huge amount of content.

So we will be able to realize the notion that is being driven through SCORM standards organization and the other standards communities today. Although I don't necessarily believe that the only path to this goal is through the standards organizations— there may be people who chart a slightly more controversial path that shortcuts our way to this huge, interoperable content.

Next is the idea of high bandwidth media, whether it be live video cameras or whether it be video on demand content. High bandwidth media will play a profound role for e-learning in a way that it doesn't today. The fact that you'll be able to get a video on demand, on any subject area, and have it delivered to your desktop is very important.

The other thing I think of for the future is that rather than cataloging content, we will eventually be cataloging people's expertise and interorganizationally will be able to find, receive, and pay for that expertise. The notion is that if I am having a problem in a Lotus 123 spreadsheet and I'm having a problem with a formula, that I can instantaneously get access to a spreadsheet expert who can view the problem I'm having (looking virtually over my shoulder), edit the formula, and get me going again. It's human-based, expertise-driven performance support. I think this will be a derivative of and a convergence of instant messaging, collaboration, live virtual classroom, and application sharing that will eventually shorten the time from "I have a problem" to "getting the problem solved." I think this will profoundly change the face of e-learning in the future.

5-4. Andrew Sadler

Andrew Sadler is Director, IBM Mindspan Solutions, and is responsible for IBM's e-learning business.

His stated vision and passion is "To change the way that the world learns." He has worked in the learning field for twenty-four years, and in adult education for twenty-one of those. Prior to joining IBM Mindspan Solutions, Andrew was vice president, Custom Learning Solutions at Global Knowledge Network, Inc. in Burlington, Massachusetts. He has also held a number of education-focused positions in the United States and Europe at Digital Equipment Corporation and International Computers, Ltd.

Question: What do you see as the impact of e-learning on companies and enterprises?

Andrew Sadler: I think we need to frame this in terms of the underlying goal that organizations are trying to achieve through e-learning. We don't do learning, e-learning, or training, or whatever one wants to call it, as a means to itself. As least we shouldn't. There should be some underlying business goal—and for most organizations, that goal is usually improving employees' time to performance, or time to competence. Our customers ask, "How do I get somebody up to speed on something in the most efficient way possible?" There are times when we want to transfer skills, times when we want to transfer knowledge, and times when we want to change behaviors.

They're finding that e-learning alone is not necessarily the single solution that will enable them to achieve these goals. This is particularly noticeable when you get out of the technical realm. If you are doing IT training, the bulk of the content is knowledge-based, and it's pretty easy to deliver that training through a combination of self-paced learning, simulations, utilizing a mentor, and so on. But when you get into soft-skills management, it becomes more challenging. Even though you can very effectively perform knowledge transfer and give people practice using technology-based training, if you are teaching something like negotiation skills and you want to ensure the skills are acquired, then it's preferable to have them sit eyeball-to-eyeball with someone else and practice. If you are not in the same room, you don't smell the fear while you're negotiating. Simulation technologies are not quite there yet!

What we've found is that blended learning solutions, which combine technology-delivered and non-technology-delivered learning, provide the best results. As I've said, sometimes delivering courses in a face-to-face environment makes the most sense. And when delivering learning via technology makes sense, there are a variety of ways to deliver that learning. We developed the IBM 4-Tier Learning Model as a way to think about this:

> Tier 1: Learning from information by reading, seeing, and hearing new material
>
> Tier 2: Learning from interaction by trying and practicing basic skills
>
> Tier 3: Learning from collaborating by discussing materials with others through chats, team rooms, and interaction with instructors on-line
>
> Tier 4: Learning from "collocation" through classroom experience and in-person interaction

Bottom line, e-learning offers ways to deliver learning much more efficiently than we could before, but it's only part of the solution.

Other examples of how organizations are realizing benefits from e-learning today are their use of e-learning to communicate with their partners, customers, and the entire supply chain; to provide training to new hires, or to provide enterprise-wide training on new applications or new systems; and to deliver courseware that can be tracked and managed so that government regulations for certification and training in health and safety areas are met.

Question: Do you think the impact is something to look for now, or is it still in the future?

Andrew Sadler: Both. Look at an example like the IBM management development training solution, called Basic Blue. It was traditionally a one-week classroom course. Implementing e-learning as one of the delivery modes of Basic Blue gave us a chance to take a new look at how we were expecting managers to acquire necessary skills. When we really looked at what we were expecting managers to learn, we realized that we actually had five weeks of material to get across in a meaningful way. Instead of saying, "That's not going to work," you say "What's the best way of delivering those five weeks of material?" And you discover that you can deliver about 75 percent of that content remotely via e-learning, bringing managers physically together at a point in time when their face-to-face interaction will have the most impact.

So business impact is being realized today, but the benefits will grow as people realize that they can do more with less and still achieve better results. Innovative enterprises are using e-learning today as an integral component of business initiatives. These successes are leading to the emergence of enterprise-wide e-learning infrastructures that will spread the benefits of e-learning throughout the organization. I think we'll see the integration of e-learning with strategic business initiatives becoming more and more common.

Question: Can you tell us about a specific company where you know e-learning has been implemented?

Andrew Sadler: Actually, IBM comes immediately to mind. Basic Blue for managers is a good example of a successful implementation of a blended learning solution, with significant e-learning elements. Three years after its introduction, we are still asked to speak at conferences about Basic Blue, have won numerous industry awards for its implementation, and work with our customers around the world who are asking us to deliver the same kind of program for them.

A second example is IT training—something IBM has a long

history of providing. While, in the past, students have traditionally attended a five-day face-to-face technical class, we're finding that self-paced training modules, virtual classroom sessions, hands-on remote labs, and access to a subject matter expert for getting questions answered provides the same result. I think you'll see some best-in-class IT training emerging from IBM.

Another good example inside IBM is the sales enablement program that used Web lectures to train the 25,000-person e-business sales force in less than forty-five days. That's very hard to do using conventional classroom methods—and is a great success story. Just think of how much time, travel, expense, and loss of productivity would be required to train 25,000 people using a traditional approach. Using e-learning to train your sales, marketing, and services organizations when a new product is rolling out makes a lot of sense—and provides a significant ROI.

Question: With regard to e-learning, do you think the impact on medium- and small-size companies is different from that on large companies?

Andrew Sadler: To some degree, yes. In programs that are focused on a company's specific business problem and require a custom approach, the economies of scale are an immediate consideration. In general, the fixed startup cost of developing a program is about the same, no matter what the size of the organization. It's more difficult for a small company to get the immediate return on its investment than [it is for] a company with a significant number of employees dispersed across the globe. The difference is less marked where off-the-shelf solutions can be used, but the business benefit is usually lower in these too.

I think it's important for companies to understand what their likely return on investment really is, because it will mitigate against certain approaches. It's very powerful to be able to provide customized training for your sales force in self-paced mode so they can carry it around on their laptops, but if you only have eight salespeople, this type of investment will probably not make good business sense. On the other hand, assuming the eight salespeople are spread all over the country, for a modest investment you provide them with a Web-based live virtual classroom instead of flying them all over the country to get them together for training, enabling you to conduct training on a more regular basis.

Question: How should companies get started with e-learning?

Andrew Sadler: "Think big, start small, grow fast."

The thought here is to apply a systems thinking approach, so you know where you want to be at some future point. Think about the state you want to arrive at two or three years down the road. This may not be your final destination; it doesn't need to be exact, and it doesn't need to be fixed, but it gives you a general direction towards which to aim. This always reminds me of the Yogi Berra line: "You better be careful when you're going somewhere, because you might end up somewhere else."

Envision a big picture of your ultimate goal. Then figure out what the first couple of steps in that general direction need to be. Pick out something that is both bounded and will have a high positive impact when successful. Select a project that will show return on your investment so you'll realize concrete results. When you can demonstrate the business benefit, it's much easier to get to the next level of investment, and then to the next level of investment, until eventually you get to the point where you're ready to convert everything. If you've been smart, your final step is not a huge change, just pulling together everything that's been done along the way.

Question: Are you aware of any well-known pitfalls that companies should watch out for as they get started with e-learning?

Andrew Sadler: The major pitfall is trying to jump to the final objective without taking the necessary incremental steps to get there. There have been a few people who have been successful taking this approach, but many fail.

What usually happens is that an organization decides to put in a brand-new infrastructure in order to deliver e-learning. This means implementing an LMS as the very first step—a rather daunting task. A goal is set to, say, deliver 80 percent of all content via e-learning within a year. But what happens in most cases is that delays are inevitable. For example, consider the process of acquiring an LMS—there's usually a fairly formal method for purchasing a large piece of infrastructure in a corporation. After six months or so of evaluation, a vendor is selected, followed by a couple of months to negotiate the contract. So it's six to nine months before implementation is commenced. An enterprise-wide software implementation can take six months or more. With even a very aggressive, fast-moving company, you're a year or more along before the software is installed. Somewhere along the way, budgets get cut, recession comes along, a sponsor leaves, and people start asking "Why are we doing this?" and "What have you done for me lately?"

I see a lot of implementations get stalled or canceled in this way. It's reminiscent of what was experienced by many when the first ERP implementations failed—there are not a lot of large-scale ERP implementations that happened seamlessly the first time through. Almost all of them were delayed, canceled, or put on hold, and then restarted. I don't suggest that e-learning is of quite the same complexity or scale as ERP, but it is of the same nature.

Question: Have you taken e-learning courses yourself? What was your experience?

Andrew Sadler: My experience has been mixed. I've taken some e-learning that's been very engaging and worthwhile, and some that's been really boring.

For example, some e-learning curricula—especially those that came out three to five years ago—simply asked me to read a book online. Why would I want to read a book on a computer screen? There's no advantage to that.

I think what's happened over the last two years is that the general quality of the content has improved significantly. And that's the result, I believe, of lessons learned from a number of failed implementations. About five years ago there was a movement, particularly in IT training, that said "You don't have to do this anymore . . . just buy a large library of courses and stick it up on your network, give it to everyone, and you're all set." And that didn't work for the vast majority of people.

What I see today is much better instructional design and production values that encourage me that we are headed toward much more engaging and higher-quality content.

Question: If you were sharing a taxi to the airport with a CEO of a company who wanted your recommendations about e-learning, what would you tell that CEO?

Andrew Sadler: If the CEO says to me "Should I use e-learning in my company?", I would say "Yes, but take the time to figure out why and how." The best way to figure this out is to engage somebody that understands the big picture of e-learning, who can look at your specific environment and business requirements, and who can then make recommendations about how to get started, how to grow, and where you should end up.

I would also make the point that the big picture can be entirely different with e-learning. E-learning can give your workforce the training it needs to be successful in a just-in-time fashion, just when it needs it. E-learning liberates you from the traditional event-based training approach and, when used appropriately, improves your business results.

Question: If you were to look ten years into the future, what do you think the e-learning situation will be like in companies?

Andrew Sadler: First of all the "e" will have disappeared entirely. We won't be calling it e-learning anymore.

As a general trend we're going to see training much more tightly integrated and imbedded into work processes. Also, the fields of learning and knowledge management will have completely converged by that time.

Here's the situation I see happening—as an employee, I reach a point in a work process where I can't proceed because I don't know something or I don't have the necessary skill. At that point, in this future scenario, I will be able to call up a variety of interventions that will help me past the sticking point. It may be a formal learning object where I can go off and learn about the topic, or it might be an informal intervention where I read a document or ask an expert for help. And that somebody I ask may or may not be a real person—it could be a computer avatar. If, for example, Joe is the only person who knows how to do something, then Joe is going to get a lot of questions. But if we can capture Joe explaining his answers to somebody else, using a combination of knowledge management and AI techniques, then we'll be able to present that in an engaging way to someone else seeking the same answer in the future. All of this will be integrated seamlessly into the workplace just like the help function in a word processor today.

That gets us back to the "time to performance" that we started with. If I'm a CEO and my employees never have to take another training course, that would be a good thing. If I never have to provide formal training for them, that would be a good thing. I can simply provide them "just-in-time learning interventions" so they get the help they need embedded into their workplace processes. Then I start to wonder, "Wouldn't it be good if the people I'm hiring from the schools and universities were prepared to work this way?" I think this will start to have an impact on our educational systems. But it won't replace the traditional education system until we figure out how to deliver keg parties, find your life mate, and all the other nonacademic activity that schools and colleges provide as they teach you how to learn. More work for the simulation technologists!

5-5. James Sharpe

James Sharpe is Director of E-Learning Technology in IBM's Learning Services group. He is currently responsible for leading IBM's Worldwide E-Learning Technology Strategies and Worldwide E-Learning Technologies Competencies. Mr. Sharpe joined IBM in January 1991 as a services consultant.

Question: What do you see as the impact of e-learning on companies and enterprises?

James Sharpe: It's all about a company's ability to quickly adapt to business changes. I see e-learning as a change agent, allowing a company's employees a way to pick up new ideas, new approaches, and new skills, in a faster way. This gives the company a competitive advantage.

I've seen this happen in IBM with our e-business transformation initiatives. IBM used technologies and techniques that were unheard of even seven or eight years ago. It allowed IBM to quickly take a significant mindshare and marketshare in that space.

So, I think the single most important impact is speed. Let me be clear about what speed gives you. It gives you the ability to capture share and increase the market value of a company and drive revenue and profit.

The other impact is cost savings. In the early days of e-learning, that's all that people were looking at. They were looking for a less expensive way of doing what they always did—and I think it's still a valid component; however, not the primary one. It's poor form to use the financial impact as the only way of showing the impact of e-learning.

Now to the impact on the people. I think it has allowed employees to increase their personal worth and allowed them to stay employable. And in some cases it even helps them pursue significant skill building without much impact on their personal lives, especially in terms of travel.

Question: Do you think the impact is something to look for now, or is it still in the future?

James Sharpe: I think the impact is absolutely available now. It's about the rate and pace that these e-learning systems can be deployed and integrated into the normal workflow of an individual.

We are already doing that now. And it's only going to get better—better results, more efficient, with better fidelity for the learning.

Question: Can you tell us about a specific company where you know e-learning has been implemented?

James Sharpe: As far as the adoption of e-learning, there are companies in the insurance industry that are really, really focusing on self-directed e-learning. They have made a commitment to produce that kind of e-learning in-house and in volume for training their employees.

At the other extreme is the IBM management development solution for e-learning that is much more of a blended approach, with instructors, with collaboration among students, and with self directed learning all mixed together.

Another example deals with a popular computer manufacturer; that example is interesting because of their consumer touch. They are proving that they can combine physical locations with a subscription-based e-learning model. They can get customer loyalty and market share by leveraging e-learning for the consumer.

Question: With regard to e-learning, do you think the impact on medium- and small-size companies is different from large companies?

James Sharpe: I definitely think there is a difference. The small- and medium-size businesses are less focused on custom/tailored solutions and are more focused on the ability to find catalog offerings that provide good instructional return from a skilling standpoint. I also think that small- and medium-size businesses are much more in tune with informal learning, and with facilitation and that kind of collaboration. They are often collocated and they're in an environment where they don't have the same kind of volumes as the large companies.

On the flip side, with large companies there is a great advantage in doing this kind of informal learning if you can get a large organization to act like a small organization. And large organizations obviously have the size to justify custom programs around their products or other business initiatives.

A small- or medium-size company that picks up on accelerating ways to collaborate will accomplish changes more quickly than large organization. However a large organization will be able to implement more formal systems to find experts and collaborate with them. There will be less of a distinction on what they can do, but more of a distinction on how that gets accomplished.

Question: How should companies get started with e-learning?

James Sharpe: If I were hired to get e-learning started for a company, I'd first start looking for the low-hanging fruit, the first hit that proves the model. If you're just getting started then that means that you've already had some false starts or there have been some things that have prevented you from getting into this pervasively. I wouldn't first try for the "end all, be all" but try to quickly show the applicability of the approach.

The other thing I would do would be to keep a balance and make absolutely sure that the skills being addressed actually generate business value. And this is hard to do. I'm not talking about an automated skills-management system, but really meeting with the business people and making sure that the programs being developed have high, immediate business value. And if not, don't do it.

Those are the two things I would do—I would say find your easy hit to prove out the model, and then evolve that to three or four key high value initiatives that have very high business impact.

Question: Are you aware of any well-known pitfalls that companies should watch out for as they get started with e-learning?

James Sharpe: I think the pitfalls are less so now that the market is getting more experienced with e-learning. But for the uninitiated, the common pitfall is the too-heavy emphasis on self-directed e-learning modules and too little emphasis on the connection between the people who know and the people who don't know.

What you have to avoid is building a large mass of self-directed e-learning content, putting it out there and hoping everyone finds it and gets it.

Make sure that what you do has business value, make sure it's accessible, and make sure it's in a volume that keeps it relevant. Don't just buy a big library of e-learning content and just put it out there.

Question: Have you taken e-learning courses yourself? What was your experience?

James Sharpe: Yes I have, but most of the e-learning courses I've actually taken have been of the self-directed type. I actually learned a lot of the IBM office applications with the self-directed e-learning available at that time. And I continue to use informal learning collaboration.

One of my ongoing goals is to take more of the collaborative e-learning courses to see first hand the pluses and minuses for myself in that environment. I wish the IBM management development e-learning program had been available for me when I first became a manager.

Question: Do you think it's important for the upper management of a company to have first-hand experience with e-learning?

James Sharpe: Even though you might think "of course they need to experience e-learning," it's really not the most important thing.

What's important is executive sponsorship for e-learning. If the only way you can get buy-in to the approach is to actually have the executive experience it, then that's when it's important for the executive to see it. But if the executive supports the business initiative of e-learning, that's what you're really interested in.

Question: If you were sharing a taxi to the airport with a CEO of a company who wanted your recommendations about e-learning, what would you tell that CEO?

James Sharpe: I'd start with "What keeps you up at night?"

Prior to the recent downturn of the economy, one of the key things that CEOs were worried about was talent, keeping good talent and attracting new talent. At the moment, however, it seems to be getting the most out of the people you already have.

Depending on what he says keeps him up at night, I'd explain how e-learning can help him get a better night's sleep. I'd explain how e-learning solutions can attract talent, retain talent, help gain share, train your partners, train your channels, or train your customers in a way that can really differentiate your business.

I would end with the cost ramifications. It's much more important to look at the business pain, and make sure that the problem he's having is really a training problem.

Question: If you were to look ten years into the future, what do you think the e-learning situation will be like in companies?

James Sharpe: I see a merger of university and corporate training. I see companies actually giving degrees, in partnership with universities. This is much like how corporate research partnered with universities in the 1940s and 1950s. The facilitation between those institutions will be of a higher fidelity because of the technology.

I think that the merger of professional education and higher education will just become stronger. The behind-the-scenes technology will be more utility-like, the technology will be semicommoditized, and what will remain as high value will be the expert and relevant content (not the volume of content, but the relevance of content) that can be leveraged across both the corporate and the academic space.

Corporate education in its role of attracting and retaining employees will still be important, but it will be much more in cooperation with the higher education space.

What I mean by *utility-like* is this. What's going to happen is that the technology will turn into a reliable set of services that will level the playing field on the technology side for almost all the players. This will provide a stable and robust platform, and by this I mean a utility kind of environment, for learning transactions and learning interactions to occur. So the environment becomes more commoditized from a utility standpoint.

But the competition around content and expertise will always be there. The content will not be commoditized. The only content area that will be commoditized will be in the 100 percent self-directed content. That will be a battle of efficiency and landing good authors. The case study for that is MIT, which put much of its course content online, but still turns away thousands of people each year who want to go to the university.

So any content commoditization will be only around the lower-tier, self-directed content, which will turn more and more into free content. The online collaboration with experts will be the real value.

CHAPTER SIX

What Are the Different E-Learning Styles?

GREMIO: "O this learning, what a thing it is!"
—William Shakespeare's *The Taming of the Shrew*

E-learning styles are ways to deal with the problems of scheduling and group interaction.

It's hard at 2 A.M. to get an instructor and a group of like-minded students together at a moment's notice. On the other hand, students taking self-directed e-learning courses can do so at any convenient time, but they work completely alone.

Questions and Answers in This Chapter

6-1.   What are the basic styles for e-learning?

6-2.   What is the "synchronous learning" style?

6-3.   What is the "self-directed learning" style?

6-4.   What is the "asynchronous (collaborative) learning" style?

6-1. What are the basic styles for e-learning?

❑ There are three basic styles for e-learning that depend on how the learning event is scheduled and how interaction with other people occurs.

❑ The three basic e-learning styles are:
1. Synchronous learning
2. Self-directed learning
3. Asynchronous (collaborative) learning

Tell Me More

The style of an e-learning experience is "how it feels" to the student. Do you feel that you're isolated, or do you feel that you're part of a group of people learning together? And if you're part of a group, how do communication and interaction occur?

The following summarizes the different styles, each of which is further described in its own question/answer section in this chapter.

Synchronous Learning

A group of students meet with an instructor over the Internet. They are all online at the same time while they are communicating with each other. The instructor can interact with the students. Students can interact with other students.

Self-Directed Learning

A student acts alone to work through the materials that are delivered to her over the Internet. There is no instructor or group of peer students to communicate with.

Asynchronous (Collaborative) Learning

This style blends the characteristics of the other two styles. A group of students meets with an instructor over the Internet and can communicate. But they are not necessarily online at the same time. Students interact with the instructor and with other students by leaving messages that can be responded to within a matter of hours. The student can work alone but can still communicate with an instructor and with a peer group of students.

It's important to realize that the "perfect" e-learning style doesn't exist. Each style has its advantages but also its challenges.

The following table shows how the learning styles fit with the first three tiers of the IBM 4-Tier Learning Model, described in the appendix:

Tier	E-Learning Styles
Tier 3	❑ Synchronous learning ❑ Asynchronous (collaborative) learning
Tier 2	❑ Self-directed learning (complex approach)
Tier 1	❑ Self-directed learning (simple approach)

6-2. What is the "synchronous learning" style?

❑ With synchronous learning, all the students and the instructor are "there" at the same time. This is much like the traditional classroom experience, except the "there" is online instead of being physically together.

Tell Me More

The word synchronous means "all at the same time" and refers to the gathering of all the students at the same time (for example, class starts at 7 P.M. Mountain Time and ends at 9 P.M.). This might not seem like a big problem until you start dealing with students in different time zones around the world and with students who are busy with their day jobs while they are trying to take the e-learning course before or after work.

Let's look at a typical scenario for a synchronous virtual classroom experience. You're a student learning the Java programming language. You connect to the course at 8 A.M. on Monday, and after signing in, you hear a lecture (at the same time all the other students hear it) by the instructor over the Internet. After another lecture, you have your first hands-on lab assignment to write your first Java program. You connect to the hands-on experience lab, enter your program, ask questions of the instructor and get the answers, and finally get your first Java program running. The instructor might even be able to "look over" your virtual shoulder to help you with your lab exercise, and you might be able to interact with other students (ask them questions, get responses) while you're in the virtual class.

In summary, the main elements of the synchronous learning style are:

❏ It is instructor-led.
❏ It is scheduled (synchronous). Everyone is "there" at the same time.
❏ It is collaborative. Students can "talk and interact" with each other.

The advantages and challenges of the synchronous virtual classroom are listed in the following table:

Advantages	Challenges
❏ Familiar learning model for students. Students know what to expect from a familiar environment. ❏ Instructor interaction makes it possible to strengthen learning. ❏ Student-to-student communication is possible in a variety of ways.	❏ Time scheduling. It can be difficult to get all of the students together at the same time. Pressures to continue doing normal day-to-day work are strong when the student has not physically "gone to class." ❏ Cost for instructor ❏ Network bandwidth and speed. Some of the "fancier" technologies for synchronous e-learning need wide bandwidths for video, audio, and graphic intensive simulations. Can

Advantages	Challenges
	all of your students be assured of a high-speed, high-bandwidth network connection?

At this point, I encourage you to turn to Chapter 2 and think about which of those case studies would be possible to do with the "synchronous learning" style. Then, of those that are possible, which do you think you would really do that way? Why?

6-3. What is the "self-directed learning" style?

"Self-directed learning" asks a student to act alone while working through a step-by-step arrangement of student materials. This is the "teach yourself" type of training. There is no instructor or group of peer students to communicate with.

Tell Me More

Let's look at a typical scenario for self-directed learning. We'll say you want to learn about financial planning in a corporation. You can download a training module from the Internet at any time you think is convenient. You can take a course in a catalog at 2 A.M.— it's always ready on demand. The course will typically be a "teach yourself" tutorial that guides you step-by-step through the major aspects of corporate financial planning. The tutorial might have:

- ❑ Text to read (the analog of reading a book)
- ❑ Recorded lectures to listen to
- ❑ Self-check quizzes to take
- ❑ Simulations to practice with

The key thing with self-directed learning is that the student acts alone—there are no other people with whom to synchronize schedules. The main drawback, of course, is that many people find learning on their own to be very difficult.

Advantages	Challenges
❑ Training is not scheduled. The student can take a course at any time (on demand). ❑ Some people learn best when acting alone—setting their own pace and scheduling their own training time to fit into busy schedules.	❑ There are no instructors or group of peer students to interact with ❑ Some people don't like to learn alone and depend on communication with an instructor and peer students to help them learn. ❑ Some people can't set their own learning pace so that they actually complete self-directed learning. In other words, some people have difficulty completing training courses unless there is someone like an instructor to check that they are completing the assignments on time.

At this point, I encourage you to turn to Chapter 2, and think about which of those case studies would be possible to do with the "self-directed learning" style. Then, of those that are possible, which do you think you would really do that way? Why?

In summary, the main elements of self-directed learning are:

❑ The student acts alone. There is no interaction with an instructor or with a peer group of students.

❑ The learning is not scheduled and is available "on demand" at any time.

6-4. What is the "asynchronous (collaborative) learning" style?

This style blends the characteristics of the other two styles. A group of students meet with an instructor over the Internet and can communicate. But they are not necessarily online at the same time. Students act alone to study the student materials and interact with the instructor and with other students by leaving messages that are expected to be responded to within a matter of hours. You can see that the student can work alone, but still communicate with an instructor and peer group of students.

The word "asynchronous" means "NOT at the same time" and refers to the gathering of the students and instructor in a semischeduled manner. The asynchronous course might start on Monday and end on Friday and have daily assignments. But within each day, the students are expected to do the coursework at a time of their convenience. There is not a specific time when everyone is expected to be online.

Tell Me More

Let's look at a typical scenario for an asynchronous virtual classroom experience. You're a student learning the fundamentals of being a project manager. Monday at 8 A.M. you get your first assignment, which directs you to listen to a prerecorded lecture over the Internet and then read the first chapter of the Web book that accompanies the course. You are expected to do that, in addition to completing a short quiz, by the end of the day on Monday. But you don't have to do anything at any specific time—you just have to complete it all by the end of the day on Monday. Each day proceeds the same way until the course is over on Friday. You can communicate with the instructor and with other students by leaving questions (like e-mails) at a course bulletin board. Everyone is expected to respond to messages within a couple of hours.

In summary, the main elements of the asynchronous learning style are:

❑ It is instructor-led.

❑ It is semischeduled (asynchronous). Everyone is "there," but not at the same time.

❑ It is collaborative. Students can "talk and interact" with each other by leaving messages.

Advantages	Challenges
❑ Instructor interaction makes it possible to strengthen learning. ❑ Student-to-student communication. ❑ Students can schedule their study at a convenient time during the day.	❑ Immediate communication with the instructor or other students is not possible. ❑ Students might need to wait for answers to key questions that are blocking their progress.

At this point, I encourage you to turn to Chapter 2, and think about which of those case studies would be possible to do with the "asynchronous (collaborative) learning" experience. Then, of those that are possible, which do you think you would really do that way? Why?

Chapter Summary

❑ There are three basic styles for e-learning. They differ by how the learning event is scheduled and how interaction happens with other people.

❑ The three basic e-learning styles are:
1. Synchronous learning
2. Self-directed learning
3. Asynchronous (collaborative) learning

Each e-learning style has advantages and challenges. There is no "perfect" style that is the best for all situations. Some are good for some kinds of e-learning situations, and others for others.

The main elements of synchronous learning are:

- ❑ It is instructor-led.
- ❑ It is scheduled (synchronous). Everyone is "there" at the same time.
- ❑ It is collaborative. Students can "talk and interact" with each other.

The main elements of self-directed learning are:

- ❑ The student acts alone. There is no interaction with an instructor or a peer group of students.
- ❑ The learning is not scheduled and is available "on demand" at any time.

The main elements of asynchronous (collaborative) learning are:

- ❑ It is instructor-led.
- ❑ It is semischeduled (asynchronous). Everyone is "there," but not at the same time.
- ❑ It is collaborative. Students can "talk and interact" with each other by leaving messages.

CHAPTER SEVEN

What Are the E-Learning Building Blocks?

FIRST CLOWN: "What is he that builds stronger than either the mason, the shipwright, or the carpenter?"

—William Shakespeare's *Hamlet*

Even though I realize you're a businessperson, and not an instructional designer, you still need a brief survey of the e-learning building blocks and what they can be used for. It would be the same if you were interested in constructing a bricks-and-mortar classroom building: You'd need to know that classrooms need student workspace, instructor workspace, and instructor tools like whiteboards, flip-chart pads, overhead projectors, and so on.

Questions and Answers in This Chapter

7-1.   What are the basic building blocks for e-learning?

7-2.   What are virtual presentations and lectures?

7-3.   What is virtual interaction with other people?

7-4.   What are Web books?

7-5.   What are simulations and games?

7-6.   What is virtual interaction with real things?

7-7. What are assessments and quizzes?

7-8. What is a virtual reference library?

7-9. What is student tracking and reporting?

7-10. How should you fit these building blocks together?

7-1. What are the basic building blocks for e-learning?

❑ There are only a handful of basic elements for e-learning. They include:
  ❑ Virtual presentations and lectures
  ❑ Virtual interaction with people
  ❑ Web books
  ❑ Simulations and games
  ❑ Virtual interaction with real things
  ❑ Virtual reference library
  ❑ Assessments and quizzes
  ❑ The building blocks are seldom used alone—they are usually combined for a specific learning experience.

Tell Me More

If you're going to run traditional classroom training, your basic instructional building blocks include:

❑ Instructor lectures
❑ Instructor question-and-answer sessions
❑ Group discussions among students
❑ Group projects by students
❑ Self-directed learning by the student from reading books, handouts, etc.
❑ Hands-on equipment exercises
❑ Tests and quizzes

You need something akin to the same building blocks to run an e-learning experience. The following table shows the building blocks we'll consider in this book arranged by the IBM 4-Tier Learning Model, which is described in detail in the appendix and which was used in the previous question/answer section.

Tier	E-Learning Building Blocks
Tier 3	❏ Virtual interaction with things ❏ Virtual interaction with people
Tier 2	❏ Simulations and games
Tier 1	❏ Virtual presentations and lectures ❏ Web books ❏ Virtual reference library ❏ Assessments and quizzes

Note: One building block doesn't fit in the 4-tier model: student tracking and reporting. The tracking of students is not part of the student learning experience, but it is vitally important from a management point of view.

It's important for you to realize that all these building blocks are not needed all the time. You might find that your learning situation requires only a few of the building blocks to achieve your goals. And that probably means lower costs.

7-2. What are virtual presentations and lectures?

❏ You can deliver lectures—an instructor or presenter talking about a topic—over the Internet in the same way you can deliver them face-to-face in a classroom setting.

Tell Me More

A standard education image is the instructor standing in front of a room of students and lecturing on a topic. (We're pretty sure that Plato and Aristotle taught this way.) A standard business image is similar: A businessperson using overhead transparencies or projected PowerPoint slides to describe a business situation. Many conferences are almost exclusively presentations by experts in the field lecturing to conference attendees.

You can do the same thing over the Internet as part of an education experience. You can show:

- ❑ The instructor talking while you hear her voice. (This is sometimes called the "talking head" approach.)
- ❑ PowerPoint-type slides while the student hears the instructor's voice.

For example, let's say you are taking an introductory class in statistics. The class will start off with an introductory lecture by the instructor. The class then might have daily lectures as the instructor introduces and explains statistical theory step-by-step for the students.

You have two "timing" alternatives for lectures:

- ❑ You can transmit "live" lectures. In this case, everyone has to be "there" at the same time.
- ❑ You can record the lectures ahead of time and transmit them to the students. In this case, students can view the lectures at a time that is convenient. (You can also record a live lecture and replay it later in recorded form.)

To make lectures work you need:

- ❑ A speaker who knows what he is talking about.
- ❑ Optionally, student handouts—either to help the students follow along, or for later reference (e.g., an outline of the lecture with the main points). You could send such handouts to the students electronically with an e-mail attachment, or you could put them on a Web page for students to download later.

Advantages	Challenges
❑ Can be recorded for replay on demand. ❑ Can be delivered "live" over the Internet. ❑ Familiar method for knowledge/information transfer.	❑ One-way information transfer: The instructor talks and the students listen. By itself, a lecture lacks interaction. ❑ More appropriate for knowledge topics than for skills-based topics. For example, good for transmitting historical facts. Not so good for learning to play the piano.

At this point, I encourage you to turn to Chapter 2 and think about where lectures would be appropriate for each case study. Why?

7-3. What is virtual interaction with other people?

❑ Students can interact with the course instructor in a variety of ways over the Internet—allowing them to do such things as ask questions and get answers.
❑ Students can also interact with other students taking the course at the same time—allowing them to pose and answer questions and even do group projects.

Tell Me More

In a traditional classroom, students don't just listen to the instructor. They can ask the instructor questions and get answers. They can also talk to other students and work with other students on group projects.

You can do the same sort of people-to-people interaction over the Internet as part of an educational experience.

There are a variety of ways that an instructor and student can interact:

❑ They can send instant messages or e-mails back and forth.

❑ They can leave messages at a Web page (bulletin board). This technology is sometimes called threaded discussion groups or FAQ sites.

❑ They can talk—using the telephone or using the Internet to carry the voices.

❑ They can use "whiteboard" technology where the instructor draws on a Web page that acts as a whiteboard and then lets selected students "use the pen" so the students can write on the board as well.

❑ They can use technology that lets the instructor "look over the student's shoulder" while the student is doing a lab exercise.

The same sorts of approaches can be used to let students interact with each other:

❑ They can send instant messages or e-mails back and forth.

❑ They can leave messages at a Web page (bulletin board).

❑ They can talk—using the telephone or using the Internet to carry the voices.

The thing to keep in mind with student–student interaction is that it has the same effect as students talking with other students in a traditional live classroom. It can be very beneficial if controlled and focused. Or it can be a lot of noise when everyone talks in an unproductive manner.

Advantages	Challenges
❑ Helps keep the student from feeling as if she is alone during the education experience. Helps the student feel she is part of a community that is learning together. ❑ Lets the student ask questions of the instructor.	❑ Network bandwidth will limit some technologies (audio, video, etc.) in some companies.

At this point, I encourage you to turn to Chapter 2 and think about where interaction between student and instructors, and among the students themselves, would be appropriate for each case study. Why?

7-4. What are Web books?

❑ You can provide electronic Web books over the Internet that serve the same purpose a textbook serves in a more traditional classroom course.

Tell Me More

The traditional classroom experience includes a textbook, or at least a binder of text, that the student is expected to read and understand. The textbook is useful for the education experience because reading is a fairly fast way to transmit information in bulk and because the student can read it at his convenience. In the same way, you can provide Web books as part of an e-learning experience.

A Web book might be:

❑ A series of Web pages that the student is expected to read.

❑ An e-mail attachment that the student is expected to read.

Regardless of the electronic format, a Web book is similar to a physical book in that the student is expected to start at page 1 and read page 2, page 3, etc. In fact, these Web books are sometimes called "page turners."

Let's say that you're taking an Introduction to Probability class. The first day's assignment is to listen to the first instructor lecture, then read chapters 1 and 2 in the Web book, then do the problems, which will be checked and corrected by the instructor before the next day's class. The Web book acts like the textbook in a traditional classroom course.

Advantages	Challenges
❑ Familiar approach—acts like a textbook in a traditional class.	❑ Students don't read the Web book (which is the same problem as students not reading the textbook in a traditional class).

At this point, I encourage you to turn to Chapter 2 and think about where Web books would be appropriate for each case study. Why?

7-5. What are simulations and games?

❑ Simulations and games are computer-based, dynamic models of complex real-life situations that let the student learn in an environment that reduces the penalties for mistakes. For example, the penalty for crashing a flight simulator on a simulated landing approach is a lot less than crashing a real airplane.

Tell Me More

It's very handy to use simulations and games to teach certain types of topics:

❑ Say you're in a business class learning about the dynamics of the stock market. The best way to learn about how the market works is to use a "stock simulator" that lets you buy and sell stocks and see the results of your actions quickly. Business schools typically let students compete in "corporate games" where students run their own simulated company and compete with other simulated companies in a simulated economy.

❑ Say you're starting to learn to fly an airplane. Taking the first few lessons with a flight simulator is less expensive than renting a real plane—and easier to recover from when you crash on your first landing attempt.

❑ Say you're learning the basics of the UNIX operating system. Entering commands into a UNIX simulator can be an error-tolerant way to learn from the mistakes that everyone makes when they are starting out.

The key point with simulations and games is that a complex real-life experience is modeled on the computer in a somewhat simplified fashion so that the student can try it out without breaking anything serious in the real world.

Advantages	Challenges
❑ Students get to try out a simplified version of a real-world experience. ❑ Students can try many approaches, even those that are likely to fail, without breaking anything serious in the real world. (Crashing	❑ In some cases it's too costly to create a simulation that is robust enough to be worth the effort.

Advantages	Challenges

on landing in a flight
simulator doesn't hurt anything real.)

At this point, I encourage you to turn to Chapter 2 and think about where simulations and games would be appropriate for each case study. Why?

7-6. What is virtual interaction with real things?

❑ In some cases, students can access remotely some "things" that are important to the learning experience. For example, if you're learning to be a UNIX systems administrator, you can be in one city but access a UNIX computer in another city to do your practice exercises.

Tell Me More

In a classroom, you might be learning a topic that requires you to practice on real equipment. For example, if you're learning to be a Linux systems administrator, you'll do practice exercises on a computer that's running Windows. You won't use a simulation of Linux because you can't learn enough from a simplified simulation.

The technology exists today to let a student in Kansas City do practice Windows administration exercises over the Internet at a computer running Windows in Los Angeles. However, the virtual reality technology is just emerging to let a student in New York practice changing a tire on a real car located in Atlanta—for these types of things, the simulation approach is still the better one.

Advantages	Challenges
❑ Lets the student remain at a remote location but still do practice exercises on the real thing with all its complexity intact, not a simplified simulation.	❑ The technology is still emerging for manipulating physical objects at a distance.

At this point, I encourage you to turn to Chapter 2 and think about where virtual interaction with real things would be appropriate for each case study. Why?

7-7. What are assessments and quizzes?

❑ You can easily provide testing over the Internet to be delivered before the course (pretests), after the course (posttests), or after defined portions of the course.

Tell Me More

The traditional educational experience uses testing for a number of things:

❑ To let the student know what he already knows before taking a class
❑ To let the student know what he learned after taking the class
❑ To the student's managers know whether the student learned the material

Tests can be delivered over the Internet. The student can go to a Web page, fill in the test answers, and get the results of the test immediately. Results of the test can be shown to the student, stored for later reporting to management, or both. (A problem that has to be addressed for testing over the Internet is validation of identity—you want to be sure that you're really testing the right person—and not a ringer.)

Tests come in two basic varieties, called pretests and posttests, either of which can be done over the Internet:

Pretests (Before the Class)

❑ Can be used to let students "test out" of a class. If you can show you know the material, you can get credit as if you had taken the class.

❑ Can be used to set the baseline of knowledge from which the student begins.

Posttests (After the Class, or After a Part of the Class)

❑ Can be used to show the student how much has been learned. As a self-check, the student can be told, for example, "If you didn't get 8 out of 10 answers right, you should go back through the material again."

❑ Can be used as a gate to further progress. If the student doesn't get 8 of 10 right for part one of the class, the student can't proceed to part two.

❑ Can be used to report to management which students passed the tests.

When the results of the test taken after the class are compared to the results of the test taken before the class, the student should get a sense for how much she learned.

It's important here to point out that testing delivered over the Internet has the same basic advantages and disadvantages as any kind of testing.

❑ Some students hate to be tested, regardless of whether it's over the Internet or in a classroom. Other students enjoy proving what they know with testing. So testing can be a turn-off or a turn-on, depending on the student.

❑ Some people just don't do well on tests.

❑ Tests give an indication of whether the material has been learned, but, in most cases, it is only an indication and not a precise measurement. Reporting of test results to management can be useful or problematic. There is sometimes a lot of fear in the students' minds when they are not clear about how management will be using the test results.

Advantages	Challenges
❑ Pretest: Students can "test out" of courses.	❑ Usage of posttests by management.
❑ Posttest: Students can check themselves, and management can evaluate results.	❑ Student fear of how a test is being used.
	❑ Some people just don't test well.

At this point, I encourage you to turn to Chapter 2 and think about where testing would be appropriate for each case study. Why?

7-8. What is a virtual reference library?

❑ You can provide supplemental reference information to any e-learning course by putting that information on Web pages that your students have access to.

❑ The Internet already holds a wealth of information in existing Web pages. You can use this information as "free" supplementary information.

Tell Me More

In many traditional classroom courses, the instructor will have "extra reading" that the students can do if they are particularly interested in a topic. The "extra reading" might be books at the back of the classroom, or it might be books on reserve in a local library.

However, with e-learning you have the advantage that the entire Internet is at the student's fingertips. And the Internet will have a wealth of information on almost any topic (although not all the information on the Internet is 100 percent accurate). Of course, you don't have to use only preexisting information—you can create your own supplementary information and make it available on other Web pages and add them to the links you give to students.

Let's say that you are teaching an e-learning course on Introduction to Project Management. Each lesson in the course can end with a series of Web links that take the students to Web sites and Web pages that discuss selected topics related to project management. The beauty of this is that you don't have to reproduce anything except the Web link to get the student to a wealth of information to supplement the course.

Advantages	Challenges
❑ Always available (on demand).	❑ Web sites and Web pages come and go over time.
❑ Possible to create your own Web pages with supplementary information that you can provide yourself but that is not part of the mainline course materials.	❑ It will be hard to find existing Web pages on the Internet for some topics (although it will be easy for other topics).
❑ Uses existing information that already exists on the Internet.	

At this point, I encourage you to turn to Chapter 2 and think about where a virtual reference library would be appropriate for each case study. Why?

7-9. What is student tracking and reporting?

❑ Although it's not part of the learning experience, tracking and reporting are important so you know who has taken what training courses.

Tell Me More

Although it's not very important while a student is in the midst of taking a training course, tracking and reporting becomes important to many people after the course is over. In other words, student tracking and reporting has nothing to do with the real learning that happens during the course itself.

Once the student finishes several courses, then:

❑ The student will want to "get credit" for the courses he took.

❑ The student's manager (1) will want to know which courses the student completed and (2) might want to know which courses the student started but has yet to finish.

Advantages	Challenges
❑ The student knows which courses she took. ❑ The student's manager knows which courses she took.	❑ You will need an automated system to track and report on student learning unless you are dealing only in very small volumes.

At this point, I encourage you to turn to Chapter 2 and think about where student tracking and reporting would be appropriate for each case study. Why?

7-10. How should you fit these building blocks together?

❑ The building blocks for e-learning do not fit together in just one way. You can use some or all of the building blocks for a specific e-learning solution.

Tell Me More

You can fit these building blocks together in almost any way you want. You can mix and match. What you do will depend on:

❑ Your training situation

❑ The technology you have available
❑ Costs

The following set of tables is a quick summary of the building blocks used in the various case studies from Chapter 2. From these tables you should be able to see that "one size" and "one design" doesn't fit all.

Case Study 1 from Chapter 2: Product Sales Update Training

Train salespeople in many countries around the world on your new product so they can start selling right away.

	Used in Sample Solution from Chapter 2
Virtual presentations and lectures	X
Virtual interaction with people	X
Web books	
Simulations and games	
Virtual interaction with real things	
Virtual reference library	X
Assessments and quizzes	X

Case Study 2 from Chapter 2: Technical Certification Training

Provide ongoing training for hundreds of company engineers so they maintain their technical certification.

	Used in Sample Solution from Chapter 2
Virtual presentations and lectures	X
Virtual interaction with people	X

	Used in Sample Solution from Chapter 2
Web books	X
Simulations and games	
Virtual interaction with real things	
Virtual reference library	X
Assessments and quizzes	X

Case Study 3 from Chapter 2: Professional Competency Training

Train hundreds of employees on company-defined skills competencies such as project management, consulting, IT system administration.

	Used in Sample Solution from Chapter 2
Virtual presentations and lectures	X
Virtual interaction with people	X
Web books	X
Simulations and games	
Virtual interaction with real things	
Virtual reference library	X
Assessments and quizzes	X

Case Study 4 from Chapter 2: Business Tools Training

Train hundreds of employees on new business tools that they are required to use on their jobs.

	Used in Sample Solution from Chapter 2
Virtual presentations and lectures	X
Virtual interaction with people	
Web books	
Simulations and games	X
Virtual interaction with real things	
Virtual reference library	X
Assessments and quizzes	X

Case Study 5 from Chapter 2: Technical Skills Training

Train hundreds of employees on demand for technical skills like Java programming, data mining, databases, and so on.

	Used in Sample Solution from Chapter 2
Virtual presentations and lectures	X
Virtual interaction with people	X
Web books	X
Simulations and games	X
Virtual interaction with real things	X
Virtual reference library	X
Assessments and quizzes	X

Case Study 6 from Chapter 2: "Ongoing Professional" Training

Provide on-demand training to hundreds of employees in such professional skills as negotiating, running meetings, coaching, team dynamics, and so on.

	Used in Sample Solution from Chapter 2
Virtual presentations and lectures	X
Virtual interaction with people	X
Web books	X
Simulations and games	X
Virtual interaction with real things	
Virtual reference library	X
Assessments and quizzes	X

Case Study 7 from Chapter 2: New Salesperson Training in "How to Sell"

Train dozens of brand new salespeople each year—these new salespeople have never been in a sales job before.

	Used in Sample Solution from Chapter 2
Virtual presentations and lectures	X
Virtual interaction with people	X
Web books	X
Simulations and games	X
Virtual interaction with real things	

	Used in Sample Solution from Chapter 2
Virtual reference library	X
Assessments and quizzes	X

Case Study 8 from Chapter 2: New-Hire Training

Train dozens of new employees each year on what they need to know to be productive, contributing parts of your company.

	Used in Sample Solution from Chapter 2
Virtual presentations and lectures	X
Virtual interaction with people	X
Web books	X
Simulations and games	X
Virtual interaction with real things	
Virtual reference library	X
Assessments and quizzes	

Case Study 9 from Chapter 2: New HR Benefits Training

Train your entire employee population, around the world, on a new health-benefits plan for your company.

	Used in Sample Solution from Chapter 2
Virtual presentations and lectures	X
Virtual interaction with people	X

	Used in Sample Solution from Chapter 2
Web books	
Simulations and games	
Virtual interaction with real things	
Virtual reference library	X
Assessments and quizzes	

Case Study 10 from Chapter 2: Informal Technical Seminars

Communicate leading-edge research via informal seminars.

	Used in Sample Solution from Chapter 2
Virtual presentations and lectures	X
Virtual interaction with people	
Web books	
Simulations and games	
Virtual interaction with real things	
Virtual reference library	
Assessments and quizzes	

Case Study 11 from Chapter 2: Legal Compliance Training

Train hundreds of employees at several locations on government regulations and laws on such topics as sexual harassment, workplace diversity, and so on.

	Used in Sample Solution from Chapter 2
Virtual presentations and lectures	X
Virtual interaction with people	
Web books	
Simulations and games	X
Virtual interaction with real things	
Virtual reference library	
Assessments and quizzes	X

Chapter Summary

❑ There are only a handful of basic elements for e-learning, just as there are only a handful of basic elements that make up a traditional classroom environment.

❑ The basic e-learning building blocks include:

  ❑ Virtual presentations and lectures. You can deliver lectures—an instructor or presenter talking about a topic—over the Internet in the same way you can do them face-to-face with students.

  ❑ Virtual interaction with people. Students can interact with the course instructor in a variety of ways over the Internet—allowing them to do such things as ask questions and get answers. Students can also interact with other students taking the course at the same time.

  ❑ Web books. You can provide electronic Web books over the Internet that can serve the same purpose as a textbook serves in a more traditional classroom course.

  ❑ Simulations and games. These are computer-based,

dynamic models of complex real-life situations that let the students learn in an environment that reduces the penalties for mistakes. For example, the penalty for crashing a flight simulator on a simulated landing approach is a lot less than crashing a real airplane.

❑ Virtual reference library. You can provide supplemental reference information for any e-learning course by putting that information on Web pages that your students have access to. The Internet already holds a wealth of information in existing Web pages. You can use this information as "free" supplementary information.

❑ Virtual interaction with real things. In some cases, students can remotely access some "things" that are important to the learning experience. For example, if you're learning to be a UNIX system administrator, you can be in one city but access a UNIX computer in another city to do your practice exercises.

❑ Assessments and quizzes. You can easily provide testing over the Internet to be delivered before the course (pretests), after the course (posttests), or after defined portions of the course.

❑ The building blocks are seldom used alone—they are usually combined for a specific learning experience.

❑ Although it's not part of the learning experience, tracking and reporting are important so you know who has taken what training courses.

CHAPTER EIGHT

What Else Affects Your E-Learning Solution?

RICHARD: "That would I learn of you."
—William Shakespeare's *King Richard III*

The perfect e-learning solution is elusive. This shouldn't surprise you since the perfect solution to any business problem is elusive. Real-world factors like time and money muddy the waters.

The important point I want to make here is this: You don't have to implement the perfect e-learning solution. The perfect solution will probably cost you more than you're willing to spend and take you longer than you want to wait. You need acceptable solutions that you can get up and running so that your e-learning can return business benefits.

Questions and Answers in This Chapter

8-1.   What factors affect your e-learning solution?

8-2.   How does the *learning problem/budget* affect your e-learning solution?

8-3.   How does the *number of students* affect your e-learning solution?

8-4.   How does *student time available* affect your e-learning solution?

8-1. What factors affect your e-learning solution?

❏ There are only a handful of factors that influence how big and complex your e-learning solution will be.

❏ These are the factors you *trade off* in order to come up with an acceptable (but probably imperfect) e-learning solution.

Tell Me More

If you think of your e-learning situation as a sheet of plastic, these factors are like sets of hands grasping the edge of that sheet and pulling it in different directions. The sheet will be stretched into a final shape based on the relative strength of each pair of hands as they pull in different directions.

The following table summarizes the major factors (sets of hands) that pull your e-learning solution in different directions.

Factor	Description
1. Learning problem/budget	Does your budget match your problem—big to big or small to small? Or do you have a mismatch of small to big?
2. Number of students	Are you looking to train dozens or hundreds of thousands of students with e-learning?
3. Student time available for training	Can the students spend weeks or only a couple of hours in training?
4. Time to build	Do you have months or days to develop the training course?
5. Deadline for training everyone	Do you have a deadline to get people to a certain training level? For example, all salespeople need to be trained by September. When deadlines are a key factor, you might look closer at less than ideal but still effective solutions.
6. Long-term versus short-term shelf life	Will the e-learning training you create be good for years, or is it a one-shot deal?
7. Starting and ending skill levels	Is your training focused on new skills or on update information for people who already have the skills?
8. Need for an instructor	Do you need instructors for the training, or can you use self-directed e-learning?

Factor	Description
9. Need for collaboration	Do you need students to interact with other students? How should the instructor interact with students?
10. Measurement needs	What degree of student achievement will be satisfactory for your training? How will you be able to tell?

Each of these is further discussed in question/answer sections in this chapter.

8-2. How does the *learning problem/budget* affect your e-learning solution?

❑ Your budget is perhaps the thing that most affects your e-learning approach.

Tell Me More

Does your budget match your problem—big to big or small to small? Or do you have a mismatch of small budget to big problem? (If you only have $2,000 for a car, you're first headed toward the used car lot, not the Rolls Royce dealership.)

Your budget is perhaps the thing that most affects your e-learning approach. If you're reading this book in page order, then you've already seen a lot of how the learning problem and the cost can range widely:

❑ Chapter 2 of this book discussed how a learning problem can come in many shapes and sizes.
❑ Chapter 3 looked at the various costs of e-learning and the general shape of a cost/benefit ROI.

In general, if you have a small budget, you'll need to start looking at low-cost approaches even if that approach is imperfect. You may face the situation where you can return lots of benefits from a planned e-learning system, but you just don't have the budget to get it working the exact way you want it to right now. So do you do nothing? Of course not. If you can't solve the whole problem with your existing budget, then you take bite-size chunks of the problem and make progress. Then you take another bite-size chunk a little later.

Other times, however, what's at stake is so important that the budget is almost irrelevant. If it's a "do or die" situation for your business, then you do what you have to do. Of course, "do or die" situations don't happen too often.

You can conclude that the budget will have more of an effect on learning solutions when there is less immediately at stake than when there are critical things at stake. The following table reminds you of the range of business impact (stakes) for the case studies described in Chapter 2.

What's at Stake?	E-Learning Case Studies from Chapter 2
Immediate business impact (revenue, sales, ability to run the business)	Case Study 1. Product sales update training. Training all salespersons quickly is critically important because your company's sales revenue depends on it.
	Case Study 2. Technical certification training. Losing certified engineers means losing business.
	Case Study 4. Business tools training if the new technical tool is critical to your business. Otherwise, it's less urgent.
	Case Study 11. Legal compliance training, if the regulation compliance is critical to being able to run your business.
High business impact but plays out over a short period of time (not immediate)	Case Study 3. Professional competency training. Training will occur over months and even years, so a small delay will be only a small problem.
	Case Study 5. Technical skills training. While training is important, it could be delayed without immediate business impact.

What's at Stake?	E-Learning Case Studies from Chapter 2
	Case Study 7. New salesperson training in "how to sell." If the new salesperson can't sell, he's not doing the job you hired him for. Case Study 10. Informal technical seminars. While training is important, it could be delayed without immediate business impact.
Mostly moderate business impact that plays out over a moderate amount of time	Case Study 6. "Ongoing professional" training. While training is important, it could be delayed without immediate business impact.
Moderate business impact that plays out over a long period of time	Case Study 8. New-hire training. While training is important, many employees (but not all) will figure it out on their own, but you won't project a "caring image." Case Study 9. New HR benefits. While training is important, many employees (but not all) will figure it out on their own, but you won't project a "caring image."

8-3. How does the *number of students* affect your e-learning solution?

❑ Depending on the number of students you have to teach, you can get very different e-learning solutions.

Tell Me More

Are you trying to train dozens of students with e-learning or hundreds of thousands? You'll get different kinds of solutions depending on what you answer to that question. (In the same way, if you need to transport yourself across town, you have a certain number of transportation choices. But if you need to transport 500 conventioneers, you have another class of choices—including buses but excluding motorcycles.)

Here are some of the attributes that shift depending on the number of students you're trying to train:

Cost Considerations

In general, it will cost more overall to train more students. If you can train ten students for X dollars, then you might be able to train 1,000 students for, say, 100 times X dollars, but 100 is more than ten (even though the cost per student goes down).

Instructional Design Considerations

The fact is that the amount of instructional design effort you put into an e-learning course is a variable. You might want to spend more instruction effort if the training is going to more people.

We like to think that all learning events need to be well structured according to sound instructional design principles all the time. But the fact is that they aren't in live, face-to-face learning sessions and they don't need to be 100 percent sound for e-learning either.

Delivery Considerations

With dozens of students, you probably don't need an LMS. But with thousands of students you will. If you are training hundreds or thousands of students, then you can start thinking about putting in a robust LMS to handle the administrative end of delivering courses. You could spread the fixed cost of that LMS over the large number of students. But if you are only training a handful of students, then you'll look for e-learning solutions that don't depend on such a robust infrastructure.

8-4. How does *student time available* affect your e-learning solution?

❑ Depending on how much time students have to spend on the training, you can get very different e-learning solutions.

Tell Me More

Your employees have jobs to do, and you can't expect them to spend 100 percent of their time on e-learning (or on anything else outside the mainline path of their job).

1. The first question is whether the students can spend weeks in training or only a couple of hours? You don't want to design a training session that takes forty consecutive hours when the student can be expected to have only two hours available to spend on it. If only ten minutes are available each day, then you'll design the training to get the maximum effectiveness within those ten minutes. In that case, also, you should probably expect that the student will move slowly (or erratically) through a series of chunks.

2. The next question to ask is "How big are the blocks of time you can expect from the student?". Your e-learning should be different in feel. If the student only has minutes a day to spend on the training, then the training should be in ten- to fifteen-minute independent chunks. On the other hand, if you are sure the students can spend concentrated periods, then you can construct the course in longer chunks (forty to sixty minutes), and you can expect a student to work through a series of chunks in quick order.

8-5. How does *time to build* affect your e-learning solution?

❑ Depending on how much time you have to get it up and running, you can get very different e-learning solutions.

Tell Me More

Do you have months to develop the training course? Or only days? E-learning courses can take anywhere from one week to six months (and longer) to put together. (In general, the simpler things take less time to build.)

In general, if you have only a short time to develop an e-learning course, you'll need to start looking at simpler approaches even if those approaches are imperfect.

You may face the situation where you can return lots of benefits from a planned e-learning system, but you just don't have the time to get it working the exact way you want it right now. So do you do nothing? Of course not. If you can't solve the whole problem with your existing budget, then you take bite-size chunks of the problem and make progress. Then you take another bite-size chunk a little later.

Another approach is to overlap things by delivering parts of the course while other parts are being developed. That way, if the whole course would take three months to develop, you might develop the first part of the course in the first month, and start delivering it while the rest of the course is still under development.

8-6. How does a *deadline for training everybody* affect your e-learning solution?

❑ Depending on whether you have a deadline for getting "everyone" trained, you can get very different e-learning solutions.

Tell Me More

This is similar to the question above on "time to build," but it is not exactly the same—this is delivery rollout.

You might face such a rollout deadline in this kind of situation: You need to get all salespeople trained on a new product by launch date. (Or all employees trained on a new benefits package by the enrollment date. Or all managers trained on new business rules and processes by a certain date.)

Nevertheless, the problem here is one of time. And if you are pressed for time, you will need to accept a certain amount of imperfection.

8-7. How does *long-term/short-term shelf life* affect your e-learning solution?

❑ Depending on the expected shelf life of the courseware, you can get very different e-learning solutions.

Tell Me More

Will the e-learning training you create be good for years, or is it a one-shot deal? Will the course be valid this time next year, or will it need updating?

❑ *Short-term shelf life:* This is training that is only current for a few weeks or months. It's the type of thing that would be done in a classroom seminar or in a meeting with slide presentations. This is traditionally a pretty informal thing and your main concern is getting the information out quickly—as long as the information is not completely disorganized. Perfect instruction design is not necessary here.

❑ *Long-term shelf life:* This is training that is current for many months or years. It might be training in your product's manufacturing process, in your company's HR practices, or in how to be a Java programmer. In this case, you are concerned with good instructional design, and you'll expect that there will be good instructional design in the course. I strongly suggest that you use professional instructional designers for long-shelf-life courses. Many companies do this sort of work. (IBM provides course design and development services that you can take advantage of.)

In brief, if the shelf life of your course is short, then you can feel OK about taking short cuts, using simple approaches, and doing low-cost course development. But if your course has a long shelf life, then it's best that you do it as well as you can from the start.

8-8. How do the *starting and ending skill levels* affect your e-learning solution?

❑ Depending on the starting skill level of the students and the ending skill level you need, you can get very different e-learning solutions.

Tell Me More

Let's say you're trying to teach the new extensions to the html

Web-page language. Your approach to that training will be greatly influenced by the starting skill level of your students. The students in your course:

❑ Might be html experts already.

❑ Might know a little html but are computer professionals who know other computer languages.

❑ Might not know html and are not computer savvy.

Then your solution will be influenced by the ending skill level you're looking for:

❑ Awareness. "Knows about" but cannot perform.

❑ Can perform with assistance.

❑ Can perform without assistance.

❑ Can perform as expert.

Clearly, if you are starting with an expert skill level and you need to train to the expert level on the new language extensions, then you have one kind of training problem. In that case, you might be able to do a short "update workshop" that could be done in a half day. On the other hand, if your students are not even computer savvy, and you need to turn out experts, then you're looking at weeks of intensive training.

8-9. How does *needing an instructor* affect your e-learning solution?

❑ Depending on whether you need an instructor, you can get very different e-learning solutions.

Tell Me More

Yes, it is always better to have an instructor. And it would be better yet if you had the best instructor in the world all the time too. Instructors can play a crucial role in training, the same role they play in classroom training. Instructors help keep the students focused, help keep them on track, and help motivate them.

Given that,

❑ You need to realize that instructors are a cost element. Almost all instructors expect to get paid one way or another for teaching courses.

❑ Also, instructors can be hard to find—some courses need instructors with very specialized skills.

❑ Finally, instructors are a scheduling constraint. An instructor can handle dozens, but not hundreds, of students at a time.

You don't always need an instructor with e-learning, but if you do need an instructor to make the training effective, then you should by all means get the instructor. Think of it this way: There are hundreds of books on "how to learn to play the piano." But most people who want to learn piano don't go to the bookstore and try to teach themselves. They go to the nearest piano teacher and take lessons.

8-10. How does the *need for collaboration* affect your e-learning solution?

❑ Depending on whether you think you need collaboration, you can get very different e-learning solutions.

Tell Me More

In general, it's good to have the ability for students to interact with other students while they take the course. This is called *collaboration*, and it simply means that one student can talk to another. It's the analog of talking to the student in the seat beside you when you're in a classroom.

Collaboration can get more involved than just talking. In a classroom, you sometimes want students to break into small teams, solve a problem, and then report back to the full class. That's collaboration too.

If you need such collaboration, then your e-learning delivery system (or LMS) needs to be able to support this collaboration. It might be implemented by:

❑ Students posting messages to a bulletin board or threaded discussion page.

❑ Students using an instant messaging function to send real-time messages back and forth.

❑ Students using "voice over the Internet" to talk.

❑ Students using video cameras to send pictures.

The question you have to ask is how much collaboration is enough. Think in terms of classroom courses you have attended: In some, it was crucial to interact with the other students, but in others you might never have spoken to another student because it was designed as a lecture class.

In short, collaboration is always a good thing because having others to talk to can help the students focus, help keep them on track, and help motivate them.

However, you do need to look at how much you really want to spend on collaboration in order to make a course more effective.

8-11. How do *measurement needs* affect your e-learning solution?

❑ Depending on what you need to measure, you can get very different e-learning solutions.

Tell Me More

As a businessperson, you're interested in e-learning because it can have a positive effect on your business. So you're going to want to know whether that's happening. You're going to want reports that tell you what's going on and whether the goals you established are being achieved.

Some of the things you might want to measure with e-learning are:

❑ Who's taken what courses?

❑ Are the new skills or new knowledge actually being learned?

❑ Are the new skills or new knowledge making a business impact on the job?

If you're only training a few people, then you can handle this manually. But as you start to scale up with your e-learning usage, keeping all this straight will quickly become complex. And you will need an automated assist to manage this complexity. You will need a learning management system (LMS), which is an e-learning application that helps you manage the entire e-learning environment (including reports).

Note: Chapter 9 of this book goes into greater detail about the capabilities of learning management systems.

So if measurements are important, you will almost by definition want to think of your e-learning solution within the context of an LMS.

Chapter Summary

There are only a handful of factors that influence how big and complex your e-learning solution will be. These are the factors you *trade off* in order to come up with an acceptable (but probably imperfect) e-learning solution.

The following factors pull your e-learning solutions in different directions:

Learning problem/budget
>   Does your budget match your problem—big to big or small to small. Or do you have a mismatch of small to big?

Number of students
>   Are you looking to train dozens or hundreds of thousands of students with e-learning?

Student time available for training
>   Can the students spend weeks or only a couple of hours in training?

Time to build
>   Do you have months or days to develop the training course?

Deadline for training everyone
>   Do you have a deadline to get people to a certain training level? For example, all salespeople need to be trained by

September. When deadlines are a key factor, you might look closer at less than ideal but still effective solutions.

Long-term versus short-term shelf life

Will the e-learning training you create be good for years, or is it a one-shot deal?

Starting and ending skill levels

Is your training focused on new skills or on update information for people who already have the skills?

Need for an instructor

Do you need instructors for the training, or can you use self-directed e-learning?

Need for collaboration

Do you need students to interact with other students? How should the instructor interact with students?

Measurement needs

What degree of student achievement will be satisfactory for your training? How will you be able to tell?

CHAPTER NINE

Developing and Delivering E-Learning

> HORATIO: " . . . all this can I truly deliver."
> —William Shakespeare's *Hamlet*

There are two dimensions to e-learning:

1. Developing the courseware
2. Delivering the courseware to the students

This chapter gives you insights into those two dimensions.

Questions and Answers in This Chapter

9-1. How do you get e-learning courseware?

9-2. Can you create e-learning courses without professional instructional design?

9-3. What is a learning management system (LMS)?

9-4. Are all learning management systems the same?

9-5. What are the steps for setting up an e-learning system?

9-6. What do you have to maintain in your e-learning system?

9-7. What are e-learning standards and why should you care about them?

9-1. How do you get e-learning courseware?

❑ You can buy e-learning courseware ready-made. This is the "off-the-shelf" approach.

❑ Or you can develop it yourself (or pay someone to build it for you). This is the custom-built approach.

Tell Me More

If you need to have your employees learn something, like project management, over the Internet, there has to be a project management course that they can get to. Where do you find those courses?

You have two choices for getting e-learning courseware:

1. *Buy it "off-the-shelf."* This means you use a course that's already been built. In the case of project management, you find a course that teaches "pretty much" what you want your employees to learn.

   ❑ You might buy the course so you can put it on your company's Internet infrastructure.

   ❑ Or, you might "lease access" to the course, which often means that the course is made available to your employees, but you don't actually store it in your company's infrastructure. Your courseware in that case will reside "somewhere else" on the Internet.

2. *Develop "custom-built" courseware.* This means you start with the proverbial "blank page" and build the course from scratch (or you might be modifying an existing course to make a custom version). With this approach, you can make sure the course teaches exactly what you want it to.

   ❑ If you have your own staff of instructional developers, you can construct the e-learning course on your own.

   ❑ Or, you might want to contract with an outside firm whose core business is designing and developing e-learning courses—and that firm will build the course to meet your specifications.

The following table summarizes the major pros and cons of each approach:

Approach	Advantages	Challenges
Custom-built courseware	Built to meet your exact instructional objectives	Can be more costly than buying off-the-shelf courseware Will take time to build
Off-the-shelf courseware	Can be ready for you to use almost immediately	Might not teach exactly what you need

9-2. Can you create e-learning courses without professional instructional design?

❑ You can feel confident about doing informal training without professional instructional design.

❑ But if you're after formal training, you're making a big mistake if you really don't know how to make an instructionally sound course.

Tell Me More

Most education professionals will tell you that you get the best student results if you:

❑ Have a professional instructional designer create the structure of the course.

❑ Have a professional course developer actually construct the course.

And that's absolutely true. You do get the best results with skilled instructional designers planning your courses and with skilled e-learning developers building the courses.

But what if you're going to do informal training—say a peer workshop or a presentation? My answer is that in most cases you can develop informal training by yourself. But, let me be clear: If you're going to train hundreds of employees in a key skill that's critical to running your business, you absolutely need a superior instructional design. In that situation, you don't want a do-it-yourself approach. You need the best results you can get.

How about the mechanics of getting informal training into the right format and onto the training Web site from which it can be delivered? The easiest way to do that is to buy a service that lets you accomplish "do-it-yourself informal training." IBM, in fact, has such a service called Web lectures, where you can create a set of PowerPoint charts, upload them to a Web site, use a telephone to record the voice commentary for the slides, and have it all ready for students to start using your informal training in a matter of hours.

9-3. What is a learning management system (LMS)?

- ❑ An LMS helps you manage complexity.
- ❑ An LMS handles the administrative tasks for e-learning —things like tracking students, enrolling students, etc.
- ❑ That administrative end can become very complex if you have hundreds of courses and hundreds of students to manage.
- ❑ An LMS will automate the handling of:
  - ❑ Course catalog
  - ❑ Course delivery
  - ❑ Student enrollment and tracking
  - ❑ Assessments and quizzes

Tell Me More

If you only need to deliver a single e-learning course to a dozen or so employees, your delivery task can be pretty straightforward and simple. You sign up the employees, run the course for them, and report how things turned out.

But if you're running hundreds of courses and delivering them to thousands of employees, your delivery tasks start to become complex. Keeping all the enrollments straight becomes a complex task. Delivering the courses, especially scheduling the instructors, and keeping everything straight, becomes a very complicated undertaking. And getting reports on what's going on becomes harder and harder to do.

What you need is an automated system to help you manage that complexity. Such a system is called a learning management system (LMS). An LMS uses Web technology to help you plan, organize, implement, and control all aspects of the learning process.

An LMS helps you with:

❑ Delivering the e-learning courses
❑ Showing the catalogs of courses
❑ Tracking users and providing reports of who did what
❑ Assessing users (quizzes, pretests, posttests)

The following short sections describe the main components of a typical LMS:

Web "Portal"

This is the Web site where users go for training. Think of it as the "front door" to the LMS. It leads to the course catalog and the other parts of the LMS. It might also include things like news, communications, and promotional "advertisements" for learning in your company.

Catalog of Courses

The catalog is a description of each of the e-learning courses available. Once a user finds an appropriate course, the student can immediately select that course. Depending on the type of e-learning course, it may be possible for it to start being delivered to the employee immediately.

E-Learning Course Delivery

The e-learning courses themselves are stored in the LMS and are shown to a user from a catalog of courses. Users can usually select a course from the catalog.

Student Tracking and Record Management

This is the administrative part of the LMS that keeps track of the students. It tracks who takes what course and when. It provides reports to administrators and managers and generally handles all the back-office record keeping that you'll need.

Assessments (Quizzes, Pretests, Posttests)

Many LMSs include the ability to deliver pretests and posttests for e-learning courses. Some also include skills assessments—students can get an online assessment of their current skills as well as recommendations of courses to take to fill their skill gaps.

Many LMSs can handle the management of the administrative part of classroom training. So if your company has some courses using e-learning and some using classroom delivery, it's possible that you could install a single LMS to manage both.

9-4. Are all learning management systems the same?

- ❏ No, they come in simpler versions and in more complex versions. In the same way, all automobiles are not the same.
- ❏ Almost all LMS systems will have a similar set of "core functions." Some will have selected extended functionality that make it easier to manage certain aspects of a complete e-learning environment.

Tell Me More

This is like asking whether all automobiles are the same. And you're going to get the same answer: "yes and no."

Like most things, LMSs come in a variety of shapes and sizes. You can get small-scale LMSs or large-scale LMSs. You can get LMSs with basic functions, or you can get them with almost all the functionality you could ever think of.

To help distinguish among LMSs, I find it useful to think in terms of three levels of functional richness:

1. Core functions
2. First extension of functions
3. Second extension of functions

Figure 1 shows these levels as concentric circles.

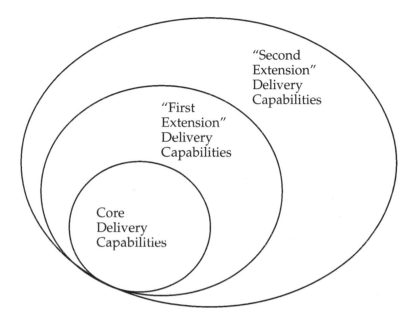

Figure 1. E-learning delivery capabilities.

(Don't be alarmed if you see LMS functions shown in different ways by different people. It's a lot like the question "How many pieces does a pie have?" You can cut it into four, six, or eight pieces, or virtually any number of pieces, and it's the same pie. I like three levels of LMS functions because it gets the point across, but it doesn't lose you in the details.)

"Core" Capabilities for an LMS

If you're going to have an LMS at all, it pretty much has to do the following things:

- ❑ Student comes to the LMS, which looks to the user like a Web page on the Internet.
- ❑ Student finds a training course.
- ❑ Student takes the training course. Courses may be in Tier 1, 2, or 3 of the IBM 4-Tier Learning Model. The course is delivered as "connect and play" via a Web browser while connected to the Internet, or as a "down-

load and play" course that the student runs on her personal machine without being connected to the Web.

❏ Basic reports are available to administrators about which students took which course and when they took them.

"First Extension" Capabilities for an LMS

If you need something fancier than the basic LMS, then these kinds of functions can be made available:

❏ Basic student testing after the course or after parts of the course

❏ Student feedback ("I liked this course"; "I hated this course")

❏ Extensive "searching for courses" capabilities

❏ More robust student tracking and report capabilities (more kinds of reporting options, to more kinds of people)

"Second Extension" Capabilities for an LMS

Beyond that, there are additional functions:

❏ Many different testing options (pretest, posttest, test out of course), possibly including certification testing support

❏ Many different administrative report options

❏ Student tracking over a long period of time through many courses

❏ A "student training record"

❏ Certificates giving proof of training completion to management

❏ Curriculum roadmap that guides students through a sequence of courses and shows how far they have progressed

❏ Personalized curriculum

❏ Collaboration with other students and/or mentors "outside of courses" in threaded discussion or chat-type pages

❏ Other: recommended next course, form for sending course recommendation to a friend, etc.

The implication, of course, is that more extensive capabilities will probably cost more to install and run. But don't let that put you off. If you have a robust learning problem, you will need robust capabilities for your solution. If you have to go to the moon, you need a rocket ship. Anything less just won't work.

9-5. What are the steps for setting up an e-learning system?

❑ Figure out what you need e-learning for.
❑ Get the system set up on a small scale.
❑ Communicate to the students.
❑ Deliver the training.
❑ See if it really works in your environment.
❑ Expand the scale.

Tell Me More

E-learning will be a change in the way your business operates, so it might be best to start small and expand in an orderly fashion.
Here are the major steps:

Step for Setting Up an E-Learning System	Comment
1. Figure out what you need e-learning for	Get clear in your mind, and in the mind of everyone involved in setting up the e-learning system, exactly what you need e-learning for. Write it down. This step sounds so simple that it's easily overlooked. More often than not, that would lead to your developing a system that doesn't do what you had (only vaguely) imagined.
	To be specific, if you need e-learning to immediately train a small but widely dispersed sales force, you'll tend towards one kind of e-learning solution. But if your problem is getting the skills of thousands of employees upgraded to a certain level

Step for Setting Up an E-Learning System	Comment
	over a period of years, you'll tend toward another kind of solution. Those solutions will be as different as a motorcycle and a 18-wheel truck, even though both are methods of transportation.
2. Get the system set up on a small scale	Some people like to wait to launch a system until the whole thing is completely ready. I recommend getting something going on a small scale even if it doesn't do everything. The advantages: ❑ Any mistakes you make will likely be small. ❑ You'll be able to recover from mistakes before the final system is launched. Maybe you're one of those people who don't make mistakes. But my experience is that systems development is something where mistakes are commonly made—there needs to be time built in to recover from the mistakes you know you'll make.
3. Communicate to the students	You need to tell the students a lot of things, including: ❑ What training they can get in e-learning form ❑ How to get to the e-learning courses ❑ Why the company is now using e-learning (instead of the old way of training) ❑ What's in it for them (in contrast to what's in it for the company) Again, the point about communicating seems obvious, but not communicating well enough with the end users is the biggest mistake that companies make when they are trying to get employees to do something new and different.

Step for Setting Up an E-Learning System	Comment
4. Start to deliver the training on a small scale	Keep the scale small to start with. You'll expand later.
5. See if it really works in your envi-ronment	Have a method for identifying and analyzing problems and fixing them quickly. Also, have a predefined measurement that tells you if you're hitting the mark or not in terms of training. If you think of your goal as a target, then you need to know whether you're hitting in the bull's-eye or on the outer ring. (Don't be one of those teams that shoot the arrow first and then draw the target later, with the arrow sticking nicely in the bull's-eye.)
6. Expand the scale	Once you are comfortable with running things on a small scale, expand the scale. Deliver more courses to more students. You might want to expand the scale in a series of steps instead of expanding from small-scale to large-scale in one swoop.

9-6. What do you have to maintain in your e-learning system?

❑ You have to update your e-learning system so it stays fresh. You have to keep courseware up-to-date, keep student access authorizations up-to-date, and periodically upgrade system hardware and software.

Tell Me More

Your job isn't over once the e-learning system is set up. You have to maintain it and keep it fresh. (In the same way, if you don't do your automobile maintenance, your car will break down much sooner than it would otherwise.)

The key things to maintain in an e-learning system are:

❏ *Courseware.* A common task required by an e-learning system is putting up new courses and taking down obsolete courses. If you are going to take a course in Ancient Greek, a course from ten years ago is pretty much the same as a new course. But if you're learning about new technologies (for example, learning to use state-of-the-art computer applications), then a course only a few months old may be hopelessly out of date. Someone has to do the job of adding new courses and taking down old ones.

❏ *Instructors.* If you are using instructor-led e-learning courses, you need to match up the right instructor skills with the right courses so you know which instructor you can schedule to teach which course. But instructors will come and go, skills for individual instructors will be enhanced, and the courses an instructor is interested in teaching will change. Someone has to do the job of keeping instructor records up-to-date.

❏ *Students.* Only certain people will be authorized to take your e-learning courses. But this list needs constant maintenance since employees come and go.

❏ *IT upgrades.* Your e-learning system is built on hardware and software that get upgraded over time. You get new, faster computers. You get the next level of the operating system. You get the next release of the LMS software. All of this needs to be managed in an organized manner.

A common mistake is to neglect to budget sufficient funds to cover the maintenance cost. (Again, you should be reminded of the person who has only enough cash for the car payments and not enough for car maintenance—you can put off the maintenance for a while, but not forever.)

9-7. What are e-learning standards and why should you care about them?

❏ E-learning standards are important because they will enable different parts from different vendors to work together.

❑   E-learning standards are still emerging.

Tell Me More

Standards are important so that things you buy from different vendors or at different times can all work together.

Think of standards like this: All Lego toys are made with the same standard-size hole so they all fit together. Electrical outlets are a standard size so that the plug fits whether you're plugging in a TV or a toaster. (Although travelers are sometimes surprised to find out that this standardization is not worldwide.)

In short, standards make it possible to interoperate and integrate. That should help you feel confident that, if your LMS from vendor A is compliant to the same standards as the series of e-learning courses you're getting from vendor B, there's a good chance that the courses will work with the LMS.

There are a number of standards that apply to e-learning, and they have acronyms to identify them like AICC (www.aicc.org) and SCORM (www.adlnet.org/Scorm/scorm.cfm). It really doesn't make sense for you as a businessperson to try to get a deep technical understanding of these standards. Any reputable e-learning vendor will be able to tell you about the standards and tell you which standards that vendor follows.

Perhaps the most important thing to say about e-learning standards is that they are still emerging. So don't be surprised if even the most reputable e-learning vendors don't follow all the standards. It's a moving target at the moment.

Chapter Summary

❑   You can buy e-learning courseware ready-made (off-the-shelf).

❑   Or you can develop it yourself (or pay someone to build it for you). This is the custom-built approach.

❑   You can feel confident in doing informal training without professional instructional design. But if you're after formal training, you're making a big mistake if you really don't know how to make an instructionally sound course.

❑ An LMS helps you manage complexity. It handles the administrative tasks for e-learning: things like tracking students, enrolling students, etc. That administrative end can become very complex if you have hundreds of courses and hundreds of students to manage.

❑ An LMS will automate the handling of:
  ❑ Course catalog
  ❑ Course delivery
  ❑ Student enrollment and tracking
  ❑ Assessments and quizzes

❑ You need an LMS when managing your e-learning system starts to become complex.

❑ LMSs are not all the same. They come in simpler versions and in more complex versions. In the same way, all automobiles are not the same. Almost all LMS systems will have a similar set of "core functions." Some will have selected extended functionality that make it easier to manage certain aspects of a complete e-learning environment.

❑ Follow these steps when implementing your e-learning system:
  ❑ Figure out what you need e-learning for.
  ❑ Get the system set up on a small scale.
  ❑ Communicate to the students.
  ❑ Deliver the training.
  ❑ See if it really works in your environment.
  ❑ Expand the scale.

❑ You have to maintain your e-learning system so it stays fresh. You have to keep courseware up-to-date, keep student access authorizations up-to-date, and periodically upgrade system hardware and software.

❑ E-learning standards are important because they will enable different parts from different vendors to work together.

❑ E-learning standards are still emerging.

CHAPTER TEN

Where Will Your E-Learning System Reside?

ANTIPHOLUS OF SYRACUSE: "Go bear it to the Centaur,
where we host,
And stay there, Dromio, till I come to thee."

—William Shakespeare's *Comedy of Errors*

Questions and Answers in This Chapter

10-1. Where will your e-learning system reside?

10-2. Why would you host your own e-learning system?

10-3. Why would you use a public e-learning system?

10-4. Why would you use private access to a shared system?

10-5. What is an e-learning utility?

10-6. Can you use multiple residencies for your e-learning system?

10-7. Why do you need to know about firewalls?

10-8. Will your company's IT infrastructure support the growth of e-learning?

10-1. Where will your e-learning system reside?

❏ Where your e-learning system physically resides is

important because it affects your costs and the way you
manage your system.

❑ You have three choices:

1. Run it on your private intranet.
2. Use a public system.
3. Get private access to a shared system.

Tell Me More

You might think that your e-learning system simply resides on the
Internet and that it doesn't really matter where the physical
machines reside. In a sense that's true—it won't matter too much
to the students who use the system. But in another sense, it will
make a lot of difference to your costs and to the way you want to
manage your system.

You have three basic choices of where your e-learning system
resides

1. *Run it on your private intranet.* If you think in terms of classroom
    training, it's like building your own education building on
    your own land. You own the building and you completely con-
    trol what happens there. You manage everything yourself.

2. *Use a public e-learning system at a Web site that anyone can go to.* If
    you think in terms of classroom training, it's like sending stu-
    dents to a college or university. You don't run the university,
    but your employees can enroll in classes just like anyone else in
    the general public. You have next to nothing to do with the sys-
    tem management.

3. *Get a "private access" shared system.* This looks to your students
    like #1, but you can reduce some costs by sharing resources
    with others. If you think in terms of classroom training, this is
    like renting a floor of an education building for your compa-
    ny's exclusive use. Only your employees have access to your
    education floor, and all the classes delivered on that floor are
    only for your employees. However, you share the building
    facilities—for example, everyone uses the same cafeteria, and
    the building overhead is shared by all tenants. You have very
    little to do with the system management.

There are pros and cons for each approach, as you'll see as you read the subsequent questions and answers for this chapter.

10-2. Why would you host your own e-learning system?

❑ If your e-learning system is installed completely within your company, you get complete control. You can, for example, connect your e-learning system directly to your HR system.

❑ You also bear all the costs and all the system management tasks.

Tell Me More

When you host your own e-learning system, it is installed within your company, inside your own firewall, on your own intranet. (Again, it's the Web equivalent of building your own education building for classroom training on your own land.) It's a separate installation of servers, software, and courseware just for your employees. No one else can access it (unless you explicitly authorize outside access). This is the way many companies today implement corporate universities.

In order to implement your own private e-learning system, you might:

❑ Build your own system from scratch.

❑ Buy commercial e-learning applications and integrate them yourself on your system.

❑ Buy commercial e-learning applications and have another firm do the system integration work for you.

The big advantage of hosting your own e-learning system is that you get complete control. The disadvantage, of course, is that you bear the entire cost of building and running the system. How these two things balance out will depend on the specifics of your situation.

Here's a quick summary of the important factors for hosting your own e-learning system.

Factor	Host Your Own E-Learning System
Courseware	You can deliver any kind of courseware: off-the-shelf courseware, custom courseware that you have developed for you, or courseware that you build yourself.
Learning management system (LMS) application	You can use an off-the-shelf LMS software package or you can build your own LMS.
Control	You have complete control of the system, which means: ❑ You control security. You can let in only employees. Or you can let in selected suppliers or customers too. ❑ You can connect your e-learning system to other computer systems and applications in your company, like your HR system. (It might take IT system integration work to accomplish this, but it's possible to do if the systems you want to connect have system–system interfaces.) ❑ All the system operating work is your responsibility. You have to maintain the IT systems, maintain the courseware, make updates as needed, and run the help desk for users.
Cost	You bear all the costs, including initial implementation, operating costs, and system updates and upgrades.
Speed to get up and running	If you're at all familiar with IT projects, then you know that sometimes they can take a long time to deliver the completed system. (Not always, but it's a good rule of thumb.)

10-3. Why would you use a public e-learning system?

❑ A public e-learning system lets anyone come and take a course (usually for a fee).
❑ This is handy if:
  ❑ You need to get some employees trained with courses that are already available at a public site.
  ❑ You need to move fast and can't wait for a private e-learning system to be built for you.
  ❑ You want to use some test subjects to find out whether e-learning will work in your company's environment.

Tell Me More

A public e-learning system is a Web site with a catalog of e-learning courses that can be delivered on demand. Anyone from the general public can come to the Web site, pay for a course (or select a "free" course), and have that individual course delivered to him right away.

Again, if you think in terms of classroom training, this is like sending students to a college or university. You don't run the university, but your employees can enroll in classes just like anyone else in the general public.

Why would you use such a publicly accessible e-learning system? For the same reasons you'd choose shrink wrap software like Microsoft Word or Excel. It already has what you need. And it's already on the shelf.

But there is another good reason to think about using a public e-learning system, at least temporarily. It's already up and running, and you can see how well your employees react to using e-learning. It won't give you the total answer about how your employees will react because the courseware might not be a perfect match to what you really need. And the delivery system might not be everything you want. But it will give you an initial feel for how e-learning can fit in your business environment.

Factor	Public E-Learning System
Courseware	You can get only the courseware that's already loaded at the public site. You can't put up your own custom courseware.
Learning management system (LMS) application	You will use whatever LMS system the public site has implemented.
Control	You don't have any control over the system, and you will not be able to connect it to your IT systems. On the other hand, you don't have any system management tasks to do.
Cost	The cost is typically a fee for each student to enroll in a course.
Speed to get up and running	It's already there.

10-4. Why would you use private access to a shared system?

❑ With private access to a shared system, you get what looks like and acts almost like a private system installed within your own company.

❑ Because you are sharing physical resources, you have reduced costs.

❑ You hand over the system management tasks to the ASP provider.

❑ Because an experienced ASP will have done this already for other customers, you can get up and running quickly and feel confident that your site will operate reliably.

Tell Me More

"Private access" to a shared system means that the Web site looks to the user as if it's a private e-learning site. The site will be restricted to a group of people: only your employees, or only your employees plus selected suppliers, or only your employees plus selected suppliers and customers. If the user is a member of this private group, she can enter and use the e-learning courses; otherwise, the user cannot enter the site.

Again, if you think in terms of classroom training, this is like renting a floor of an education building for your company's exclusive use. Only the people you authorize have access to your education floor, and all the classes delivered on that floor are for that select group of people.

These shared systems are usually hosted by an application service provider or ASP. In most cases, these ASP private sites are not separate Web site installations, but are different views into a common, underlying system. Different customers of the ASP see different courses and get different access capabilities. The underlying system, though, is common among several customers. The different customers share the system resources and services, and thus also share the costs of running the system.

ASPs have the experience and scalability to support e-learning sites. A good e-learning ASP has done all this before and has the relationships and experience to make it successful.

Factor	Private Access to a Shared System
Courseware	You can deliver any kind of e-learning courseware: off-the-shelf courseware, custom courseware that someone develops for you, or courseware that you build yourself.

Factor	Private Access to a Shared System
Learning management system (LMS) application	You will use the LMS that the ASP has implemented.
Control	You will have control of your system at the user level, but not at the system level. This means: ❑ You control authorizations. You can only let in employees. Or you could let in selected suppliers or customers. But you don't control basic security for the site. ❑ You most likely cannot connect your e-learning system to other computer systems and applications in your company such as your HR system.
Cost	You share the costs of running the system with other customers who are using the same physical resources for the system. ASPs might charge by "delivery unit" or "course access" or even by a flat monthly fee.
Speed to get up and running	Usually a matter of weeks for an experienced ASP.

10-5. What is an e-learning utility?

❑ An e-learning utility is aimed at temporary access to an e-learning system.

❑ This is much like the ASP model described in Question 10-4 except that, as with any other utility, you only plug into it as needed.

Tell Me More

An e-learning utility is something you plug into only as needed, and it aims at solving the following kind of problem.

> We Do Virtual Stuff, Inc. is implementing a new CRM system. In order for the new system to be successful, both technical and end-user training is needed. Traditionally all users would be sent to class at the end of the CRM implementation phase.

> However, We Do Virtual Stuff, Inc. is spread among many geographic locations, which leads to scheduling challenges, travel expenses, and inconsistency in content delivery of classroom courses. If the classroom approach is used, many current and future users will not get effective training, and the new CRM system will not be as productive or achieve operation targets. So this looks like a good situation for e-learning.

> But, We Do Virtual Stuff, Inc. does not yet have its own e-learning infrastructure and does not yet want to get into a long-term relationship with an ASP for a shared system.

> We Do Virtual Stuff, Inc. wants to have access to an e-learning infrastructure only for the period of time it takes to get the CRM users trained—after that, access to the rented e-learning utility can end.

In short, what an e-learning utility gives you is short-term access to an e-learning system. You only need access for a matter of months, and that's what you get. After that you disconnect. The whole goal of an e-learning utility is:

- ❑ Getting you up and running fast
- ❑ Running the courses you need
- ❑ Disconnecting you after you're done

In most cases, an e-learning utility is temporary access to a shared system run by an ASP. This means that it has many of the same characteristics as the private access to a shared system in Question 10-4 above:

Factor	E-Learning Utility
Courseware	You can deliver any kind of e-learning courseware: off-the-shelf courseware, custom courseware that someone develops for you, or courseware that you build yourself.
Learning management system (LMS) application	You will use the LMS that the ASP has already implemented.
Control	You will have control of your system at the user level, but not at the system level, which means: ❏ You control authorizations. You can only let in employees. Or you could let in selected suppliers or customers. But you don't control basic security for the site. ❏ You most likely cannot connect your e-learning system to other computer systems and applications in your company such as your HR system.
Cost	You will typically pay only for what you use. This is sometimes called "metering," or paying "by the trip."
Speed to get up and running	Usually a matter of weeks for an experienced ASP.

10-6. Can you use multiple residencies for your e-learning system?

❏ You don't have to have a single place for your employees to go for e-learning. You can send them to a combi-

nation of public sites, to your own private e-learning system, and to anywhere else you want.
❑ How you mix and match where your employees go for training will most likely depend on costs and on what courses are available at what location.

Tell Me More

At first, this question seems to be asking "What if you can't make up your mind where you want your e-learning system to reside?"

But it's really more than that. If you think in terms of classroom training, you might want to have a company education center where most of the training occurs, but you also might want to send some of your employees to colleges and universities for other kinds of specialized training. And you might want to rent a hotel ballroom occasionally for special lectures.

If we put that in terms of the Internet, you might have this situation:

❑ You have a corporate online university where most of the online training is expected to occur.
❑ You send some of your employees to public Web sites, or to other private Web sites you've gotten them access to, for certain types of training that they can't get at your online university.

Things to consider with multiple sources of education are:

❑ What e-learning courses are available at what location, and how important is it for your business to have access to those courses?
❑ The employee education record. Is it important to your company to be able to produce a single list of all the e-learning courses a student has taken? If so, then you'll have to dig into the reporting capabilities of the other sites you send students to.
❑ Cost and payment. For example, which of your employees are allowed to spend how much money taking e-learning courses from a public site if you already have a corporate e-learning center for which you have to recover the costs?

So, the bottom line is that it's possible to have many different online places to which you send your employees for e-learning. But you'll have to decide whether your specific situation balances the pros and cons of doing that.

10-7. Why do you need to know about firewalls?

❑ Firewalls are filters that keep unauthorized users and data out of your company's intranet (see Figure 2).

❑ But if students are inside your company's intranet, and are trying to take e-learning courses that are coming across the firewall from an outside Web site, you need to be sure the firewall is not filtering out the e-learning course data. If your firewalls are filtering things you don't want filtered out, the e-learning course might not work properly.

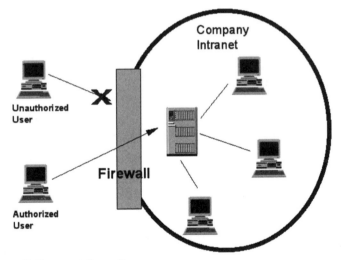

Figure 2. Intranet firewall.

Tell Me More

Firewalls exist to keep unauthorized users out of your company's intranet. Figure 2 shows what happens. Unauthorized users cannot get into the company intranet, but the authorized user can.

A firewall essentially acts as a filter. Besides filtering out unauthorized users, firewalls are sometimes set up by the company's IT department to filter out certain kinds of data. For example, the firewall could filter out files bigger than two megabytes or filter out streaming audio or filter out streaming video.

But if students are inside your company's intranet and trying to take e-learning courses that are coming across the firewall from an outside Web site, you need to be sure the firewall is not filtering out the e-learning course data. If it's being filtered out, the e-learning course won't work.

You need to be sure that the firewall is not going to filter out anything important coming from e-learning courses coming from external Web sites. Think about file size, video, audio, and any other special features of the courseware.

10-8. Will your company's IT infrastructure support the growth of e-learning?

❑ Do you have the network bandwidth to run the e-learning courses you want?

❑ Are your employees equipped with computers that let you run the e-learning courses you want?

❑ Will your e-learning system scale up to handle a large number of students?

Tell Me More

Your company's IT infrastructure includes:

❑ Networks

❑ The computers that your employees use (laptops, desktops, etc.)

❑ System and application programs and the computers on which they run (usually called "servers")

Such an IT infrastructure is a lot like the infrastructure for a city—including the electrical lines, water lines, phone lines, buildings, subways, etc. The key things to know about any infrastructure are that:

- ❏ It's expensive to set up.
- ❏ It's expensive to operate.
- ❏ It needs constant maintenance and upgrading, especially as usage grows.

In almost all cases, your company's IT infrastructure will already exist. You will not be establishing an IT infrastructure just for e-learning. You will use what's already there and being used for e-mail, running business-critical applications, and running other more mundane computer applications.

The question is whether your IT infrastructure can support the e-learning you want to run over it. There are these factors to consider:

Network Bandwidth

Network bandwidth refers to the amount of data that can get across the network in a period of time. Many people metaphorically think of the bandwidth as the thickness of the pipes in the network. I'm sure you've seen the difference yourself when you're connected to the Internet with a 28.8Kps modem or when you're connected though a high-speed line.

As your need for e-learning grows, your need for bandwidth will grow for two reasons:

- ❏ Increased traffic. More users sending and receiving more and more data.
- ❏ Increased use of video and audio, and other high-function e-learning courseware that can transmit large amounts of data. Thin pipes will limit the usage of such things as audio and video and will cause delays when downloading large files or complicated Web pages.

The question then to ask is "How big are the pipes in your company's intranet?"

The thing to be aware of, however, is that you might be able to control the size of the intranet pipes in your company, but if you're using the Internet itself, the size of those pipes is out of your hands. (Think of the times when you got the message "net congestion" when streaming audio over the Internet.) You might be surprised to know that the thickness of pipes is not uniform across the Internet—some parts have fast, thick pipes and some are slow, thin pipes.

Student Hardware

Your employees will need a computer to access the e-learning courseware, and it's probably a safe bet that they already have one for other business needs. Keep in mind the following:

- ❑ Student machines need maintenance and occasional upgrading as the state of the art moves onward.
- ❑ This goes double for computers being used by e-learning instructors.
- ❑ Some companies provide the latest in computer equipment to their employees. Some don't. If you're going to use e-learning courseware that uses the latest technology, make sure that each employee's computer can handle it. I wish I didn't know about companies who wanted to stream audio to their employees as part of a learning experience, only to find that the computers their employees had on their desks were missing the audio cards.

Also, think about whether you are expecting employees to use the e-learning courses only at the office, or from home (or on the road). What capabilities do you expect them to have at home? The most important thing to check here is the bandwidth. If many employees are going to connect with a 28.8Kps or 56Kps modem, then e-learning that sends large amounts of data is going to appear very, very slow—and ultimately annoy the students.

Scalability

Scalability is connected to growth. In general, you want a scalable e-learning system so that, whether you're teaching twenty people or 2,000 people, you do not run into technology barriers. What's a technology barrier? In the old days of personal computers, when they ran DOS instead of Windows, there was a 640K memory barrier. You could run programs as long as they fit within 640K, but after that you had problems. In short, DOS didn't scale. When things got bigger, it didn't expand gracefully to accommodate the bigger things.

In terms of e-learning, you don't want to find that your e-learning system works just fine with 100 users but breaks down if you have 500 users.

It's important to note that there are other scalability barriers besides the technology. Instructor-led courses are not scalable like self-paced courses. An instructor can handle from twenty to forty students at a time. If you have hundreds and hundreds, you'll need more instructors.

Chapter Summary

You have three basic choices on where your e-learning system resides:

1. *Build it yourself and run it on your private intranet.* If you think in terms of classroom training, it's like building your own education building on your own land. You own the building and you completely control what happens there.

2. *Use a public e-learning system at a Web site that anyone can go to.* If you think in terms of classroom training, it's like sending students to a college or university. You don't run the university, but your employees can enroll in classes just like anyone else in the general public.

3. *Get private access in a shared system.* This looks to your students like choice number 1, but you can reduce some costs by sharing resources with others. If you think in terms of classroom training, this is like renting a floor of an education building for your company's exclusive use. Only your employees have access to your education floor, and all the classes delivered on that floor are only for your employees. However, you share the building facilities—for example, everyone uses the same cafeteria, and the building overhead is shared by all tenants.

Here is a quick summary of the major factors to consider when deciding where your e-learning system resides.

Factor	Host Your Own E-Learning System	Public E-Learning System	Private Access to a Shared System
Course-ware	You can deliver any kind of courseware: off-the-shelf course-ware, custom courseware that you have developed for you, or courseware that you build yourself.	You can get only the course-ware that's already loaded at the public site. You can't put up your own custom courseware.	You can deliver any kind of e-learning course-ware: off-the-shelf courseware, custom courseware that someone develops for you, or courseware that you build yourself
Learning management system (LMS) application	You can use an off-the-shelf LMS software package, or you can build your own LMS.	You will use whatever LMS system the public site has implemented.	You will use the LMS that the ASP has already implemented
Control	You have complete control of the system, which means: You control security. You can only let in employees. Or you could let in selected suppliers or customers. You can connect your e-learning system to other computer systems and appli-	You don't have any control over the system, and you will not be able to connect it to your IT systems. On the other hand, you don't have any system management tasks to do.	You will have control of your system at the user level, but not at the system level, which means: You control authorizations. You can let in only employees. Or you could let in selected suppliers or customers. But you don't control basic security for the site.

Factor	Host Your Own E-Learning System	Public E-Learning System	Private Access to a Shared System
Control (cont'd)	cations in your company, such as your HR system. (It might take IT system integration work to accomplish this, but it's possible to do if the systems you want to connect have system–system interfaces.) All the system operating work is your responsibility. You have to maintain the IT systems, maintain the courseware, make updates as needed, and run the help desk for users.		You most likely cannot connect your e-learning system to other computer systems and applications in your company, such as your HR system
Cost	You bear all the costs, including initial implementation, operating costs, and system updates and upgrades.	The cost is typically a fee for each student to enroll in a course.	You share the costs to run the system with other customers who are using the same physical resources for the system.

Factor	Host Your Own E-Learning System	Public E-Learning System	Private Access to a Shared System
Cost (cont'd)			ASPs might charge by "delivery unit" or "course access," a flat monthly fee, or by some other "metering" scheme.
Speed to get up and running	If you're at all familiar with IT projects, then you know that sometimes it can take a long time to deliver the completed system. (Not always, but it's a good rule of thumb.)	It's already there.	Usually a matter of weeks for an experienced ASP.

CHAPTER ELEVEN

Where Is E-Learning Headed in the Future?

FLAVIUS: " . . . the future comes apace."

—William Shakespeare's *Timon of Athens*

There are lots of e-learning improvements in store in the near future and even more dramatic improvements coming in the long-term future. What we have already with e-learning can be pretty spectacular, but there's lots more to come.

Questions and Answers in This Chapter

11-1. What makes me think I can see into the future?

11-2. What's going to happen with the courseware itself?

11-3. What's going to happen "around the courseware"?

11-1. What makes me think I can see into the future?

❑ While I don't have a crystal ball, I can tell you what's likely to happen based on the evidence of other recent technologies.

❑ E-learning has a good chance of growing quickly, reaching critical mass, and changing the fabric of how training occurs in businesses.

Tell Me More

I can't see infallibly into the future, but I think we can feel pretty safe that e-learning is on the same path that many other society-changing technologies have already taken. So I'm not giving any guarantees here, but I'm talking about what's very likely to happen.

Think of how e-mail and the fax machine have changed the day-to-day workings of business. And think of how the cell phone has changed things in the larger social setting. Or think of the impact of the computer spreadsheet and the word processor.

There seems to be a curve of natural progression for these kinds of things.

First we see a few people adopting the new technological approach. A few people have a cell phone, or a few people have a computer with a spreadsheet. Then more people start using that new technology—and the technology itself improves while it gets more affordable. Then lots more people start using it, and it reaches a critical mass.

At that point, it starts to change the structure of the society and the businesses that use it. What business person today is without a cell phone? What business person is without an Internet connection or a fax machine? Who could survive anymore without the ability to conference several people together on the phone to have a virtual meeting? It even becomes hard to remember what it was like when everyone didn't have a cell phone, when everyone wasn't connected to the Internet, or when you couldn't watch 200 channels on your TV.

You can see from those examples that it's not just about the technology. It's about how the technology interacts with the social norms and changes the fabric of a business, as well as the basic assumptions that employees make as they do their work.

Like those other technologies, e-learning has a good chance of growing quickly, reaching a critical mass, and changing the structure and fabric of the way training is handled in most companies.

11-2. What's going to happen with the course-ware itself?

❑ The e-learning technology will become richer and rich-er over time so that students will get closer and closer to the richness of a face-to-face learning experience.

❑ And e-learning courses will probably get cheaper to make and cheaper to deliver.

❑ But remember that the quality of any training session is in the instructional design. It's possible to make a bad movie that has lots of spectacular special effects, and it's possible to make a bad e-learning course that has lots of spectacular multimedia and virtual reality effects.

Tell Me More

We have to realize that today we're still near the beginning of what e-learning technology is going to turn into. We're probably at the stage in e-learning that films were in around 1910. It works well enough, but it will look pretty primitive when we look back twenty-five, fifty, or seventy-five years from now.

The main message about e-learning courseware is that it will become a richer and richer experience for the student. It will become closer and closer to the multifaceted experience you can get with face-to-face learning. I can be pretty confident in predict-ing that the student experience with e-learning will become richer and richer.

Let's look at what's likely to happen to some of the e-learning building blocks described in Chapter 7:

E-Learning Building Block	Into the Future . . .
Virtual presentations and lectures	With more broadband capabilities and richer virtual reality technology, it will look more and more as if the speaker is face-to-face with the student.

E-Learning Building Block	Into the Future . . .
Virtual interaction with other people	Again, with more broadband capabilities and richer virtual reality technology, students will be able to interact with instructors and with other students in ways more like face-to-face interaction. Instead of typing messages, students will talk. And if the other person isn't online at the moment, the message will be stored and delivered later.
Simulations and games	Gaming technology will make it easier and cheaper to construct meaningful games and simulations so that they can be used in a much wider variety of e-learning courses. No longer will these be used sparingly because of the expense and difficulty of constructing them. For example, the key part of learning to sell is honing the sales skills needed to react to a buyer's questions and fears—what better way to practice them than interacting with a virtual buyer?
Virtual interaction with things	Today, you can remotely access programs running at remote computers. Tomorrow, you will be able to remotely access a wide variety of real and virtual things, which can then be used to provide hands-on experience with the subject being learned. For example, learning to drive a car can be taught via a virtual experience.
Assessments and quizzes	Today, a quiz on the Internet looks a lot like a quiz on paper: Type in the answers to these questions or select from a list of answers. But with the expected advances in virtual reality technology, a quiz could be assessing your reaction to a virtual experience, or a test could determine how well you interact with your virtual partner in a mock negotiation session.

E-Learning Building Block	Into the Future . . .
Virtual reference library	Today, most things in the library are still text-based. But the libraries of the future will be full of virtual reality "experiences" as well as video and audio recordings. Many more data formats will be available. Moreover, there will be much more information, indexed in a way that partly reads your mind to guess at what you're really looking for.

The bottom line is simply that technology marches on.

Remember though that technology is the means to the end, not the end itself. Just because you have a high-tech film with lots of computer-generated special effects, it doesn't mean you have a good movie. The quality of a movie is in the script. The quality of a training session is in the instructional design. It's possible to make a bad movie that has lots of spectacular special effects, and it's possible to make a bad e-learning course that has lots of spectacular multimedia and virtual reality effects.

Finally, it will probably cost less to deliver e-learning courses on a per-capita basis in the future since running anything on computers tends to get cheaper and cheaper. However, it's not at all clear that it will cost less to develop e-learning courses in the future. (It doesn't cost less to develop movies in 2001 than it did in 1950, especially if you're thinking of a movie loaded with special effects.)

11-3. What's going to happen "around the courseware"?

❑ The capability and flexibility of the systems that surround the e-learning courses will continue to improve, making e-learning even easier to manage.

❑ More and more e-learning systems will be interconnected, which should improve the accessibility and availability of e-learning courses.

Tell Me More

What do I mean by "around the courseware"? I mean the systems that deliver the e-learning courses and the systems that help you manage the administrative complexity of delivering hundreds of courses to hundreds of students. Today, these are referred to as learning management systems (LMSs); we looked briefly at their characteristics in Chapter 9.

The first thing is that LMSs will continue to improve. You'll continue to get better and better capabilities for managing the enrollments, course delivery, reports, upgrades, and maintenance. The emerging e-learning standards will solidify, and today's LMS will evolve into a very rich e-learning platform.

The next thing is that e-learning will probably become even more interconnected. Here's what I mean by that statement. Today, the basic model for e-learning is that you go to a specific Web site and take a course from what's available in that Web site's e-learning catalog. This is very much like going to a public library and taking out a book from what is available on the library shelves. But if we can predict anything with certainty, it is that the Internet will, over time, become an ever more closely connected web.

So the model that could emerge is what I'll call "the interlibrary loan model." I can go to my local public library and take out a book from its shelves. But I can also ask my librarian to get me a book from another library in my geographic region. So, in the future, you might see a similar thing in e-learning. You might go to one e-learning site and take e-learning courseware that is not actually available from that site but from a different site. Behind the scenes, the first site will get the course from the second site and deliver it to the requesting user. You can think of this as the "take a course from anywhere" model.

Of course, a number of business and technology problems will need to be ironed out before the "take a course from anywhere" model can be realized:

❑ *Standards.* Interconnection generally can't happen without following technology standards.

❑ *Student authorization agreements.* If you are authorized to take courses at one site, how will another site know about you? And will you get credit for taking the course back at your home system?

❑ *Payment.* If it costs money to take a course, how does the money flow when someone from another site takes a course?

None of these problems are insurmountable, but the time-frame for getting to this situation will depend on market pressures with timings that are impossible to predict.

Chapter Summary

❑ E-learning has a good chance of growing quickly, reaching critical mass, and changing the fabric of how training occurs in businesses.

❑ The e-learning technology will become richer and richer over time, so that students will get closer and closer to a face-to-face learning experience.

❑ And e-learning courses will probably get cheaper and cheaper to deliver.

❑ But remember that the quality of a training session is in the instructional design. It's possible to make a bad movie that has lots of spectacular special effects, and it's possible to make a bad e-learning course that has lots of spectacular multimedia and virtual reality effects.

❑ The flexibility of the systems that surround the e-learning courses will continue to improve, making e-learning ever easier to manage.

❑ More and more e-learning systems will be interconnected, which should improve accessibility and availability of e-learning courses.

What Is the IBM 4-Tier Learning Model?

❑ IBM's 4-Tier Learning Model is a framework for thinking about learning in a business.

❑ IBM's 4-Tier Learning Model recognizes that businesses need a variety of different delivery modes for learning. One mode doesn't fit all situations. Learning modes can range from different kinds of e-learning to traditional face-to-face classroom training.

❑ The categories of the IBM 4-Tier Learning Model include:

1. Learn from information.
2. Learn from interaction.
3. Learn from collaboration.
4. Learn from colocation.

Tell Me More

IBM's 4-Tier Learning Model (see Figure A-1) is a framework for thinking about learning in a business. IBM itself is using this model as the basis of its e-learning creation and e-learning delivery strategies, tactics, and products.

IBM's 4-Tier Learning Model recognizes that businesses need a variety of different delivery modes for learning. One mode doesn't fit all situations. Learning modes can range from different kinds of e-learning to traditional face-to-face classroom training.

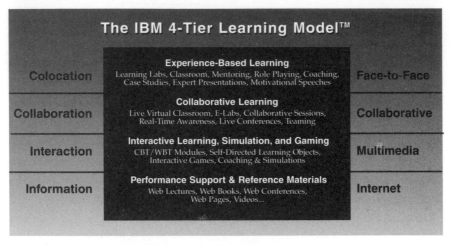

Figure A-1. The IBM 4-Tier Learning Model.

Some training situations need only simple self-review and self-study, while other training requires more elaborate capabilities like collaboration and interaction among students and instructors connected via the Internet. And some training situations are best handled with a blending of several methods. The basic premise of the IBM 4-Tier Learning Model is that there are a variety of delivery modes and that businesses have a wide variety of solutions available by using different modes or by blending the modes.

Blending the tiers: When you read the descriptions of the tiers, you might think that each tier is exclusive of the others. But the power of this learning model comes into play when you think of blending, or combining, the tiers in a single learning solution. You can blend elements from each tier, or only from selected tiers. The IBM management development training curriculum, described in Chapter 1, is clearly a blended solution.

Tier 1: Learn from Information

This tier deals with self-directed knowledge transfer. As the arrow in the Figure A-2 indicates, information flows one way from the computer to the student.

Figure A-2.

This is the Internet analog of reading a book or going to a lecture. In fact, a Web lecture is the Internet version of a PowerPoint–based presentation. This means that from your Internet-connected computer you see the slides and hear the speaker's voice as each slide is presented in turn. And a Web book is a book that you read over the Internet (usually with multimedia enhancements to the text).

This tier is ideal for the same type of training for which you would previously have used a book, presentation, or lecture. It's ideal for quick update training, new product launches, and other types of training where self-directed learning is appropriate. It's useful where you don't need complicated instructional strategies or you are only affecting a small number of students.

Examples:

❑ Sales update education can be taught using a Web book, a multimedia enhanced "book" that can be downloaded and read at the salesperson's computer or read over the Web using a browser.

❑ New technical concept training (for example, "Why Open Networks Are Important to Your Business") can be taught using a Web lecture—a slides-and-audio lecture that can be accessed via a browser.

❑ A new product strategy can be outlined in a short video feed that can be accessed from a Web browser.

Tier 2: Learn from Interaction

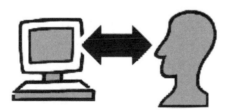

Here, information comes to the student, but the student can interact and practice as well, as illustrated in Figure A-3.

That interaction and practice capability are indicated by the two-sided arrow

Figure A-3.

in the picture at the left. The student interacts, but she interacts only with automated programs or processes—not with other students or an instructor. Student practice with Tier 2 courseware is interaction with a simulation.

Training in this tier is ideal for basic skills in new applications or for procedural tasks that do not need interaction or collaboration with other people, including an instructor, or that do not need interaction with programs beyond simulated interaction.

Examples:

❑ Product "basic training" can be taught using interactive Web pages and simulated exercises that run over the Internet.

❑ Training for a new sales tool can taught using a CD-ROM-based application and simulated exercises run from that CD-ROM.

Figure A-4.

Tier 3: Learn from Collaboration

This tier brings e-learners together online with other e-learners and also with instructors via the Internet. Collaborative techniques such as chat rooms, team rooms, and interaction with instructors online allow learners to be able to learn in collaborative groups and from their joint experiences (see Figure A-4).

Students can interact online with an instructor as well as with fellow students. E-learners can meet at the same time (synchronous interaction). Or they can meet via team rooms (threaded discussion pages) where they meet asynchronously by leaving messages that are picked up and responded to within a few hours.

With this personal interaction capability, this tier provides many of the elements of the virtual classroom.

Beyond personnel interaction, Tier 3 also enables more sophisticated distant interaction with running programs. This means a student is not restricted to interacting with a simulation of a running program, but can interact with the actual application running remotely in an e-lab environment. For example, a student learning the Websphere product in a Tier 3 course can do the hands-on lab exercises over the Internet at a remote computer that is actually running Websphere.

More Examples:

- ❑ Professional skills in negotiating can be taught using a synchronous virtual classroom where the instructor and students are all online at the same time.
- ❑ New-hire training can be taught using an asynchronous class model where the instructor and students collaborate via a threaded discussion page.
- ❑ In-depth product training can be taught using e-labs where each student has remote access to a computer running an application program in order to do hands-on lab exercises for the course.

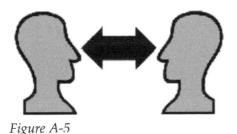

Figure A-5

Tier 4: Learn from Colocation

This means that the students are physically in the same place as other students and instructors/mentors (see Figure A-5). This is the traditional classroom model.

One very important point to remember is that technology will not replace certain key learning strategies that rely on face-to-face experiences with peers and mentors. Rather, the appropriate use of e-learning strategies enables important but costly classroom and mentoring activities to be focused on higher-level skills and behavioral change.

The strengths of the classroom are well known: Face-to-face activities provide immediate responses, allow for nuances of non-verbal cues (which many scholars argue are the most important of communications), are flexible to human needs, and can adapt as needed to different learners' styles. For developing people skills, the human interaction you can get in a classroom setting is arguably the most powerful of learning interventions.

Furthermore, there are "hands-on lab" situations where interaction with the physical item is required. For example, changing a tire on a car. Or, taking apart and repairing a copier machine for which a simulation does not exist.

Examples:

- ❑ One session of New Manager Training can be conducted in a face-to-face classroom class.
- ❑ A workshop for experienced project managers can be taught in a face-to-face classroom class.
- ❑ A hands-on workshop in computer hardware maintenance can be taught using actual hardware in a classroom environment.

E-Learning Lingo

TROILUS: "Words, words, mere words, no matter from the heart."
—William Shakespeare's *Troilus and Cressida*

AICC

An important industry standard for e-learning. See http://www.aicc.org.

asynchronous learning

A type of learning in which the instructor and students are connected, but not at exactly the same time. Instead, they leave messages for each other, and the messages are expected to be responded to in a matter of hours.

bandwidth

The amount of data that can be shipped across the Internet (or on an intranet inside a company). Often referred to as the "width of the pipes." Wider bandwidth opens the possibility of better audio, sharper and smoother video, and richer real-time interactivity.

blended learning

Learning that combines components of e-learning on the Internet with other learning technologies like CD-ROMs or classroom training or books. Taking a "blended learning" course might include using the Internet, playing CD-ROMs, and going to a short classroom experience.

bulletin board

> An Internet Web page where students and the instructor can leave messages. This provides a method of asynchronous interactivity by posting messages and replies to messages. A student can ask a question of the instructor in the morning, the instructor can answer it at noon, and the student can read the answer in the evening. Also called "team room," "chat room," and "threaded discussion."

CBT

> See "computer-based training"

chat room

> A Web page where students and the instructor can enter messages and replies in real time. Everyone signs in to the chat room at the same time, and students can type in questions and get immediate answers if the instructor is in the chat room at the moment. Students can also interact with other students in this way. (Such student–student communications can be private conversations or open for all to see.)

collaboration

> Generally refers to the way students can work together in a virtual manner in e-learning courses.

computer-based training (CBT)

> Any training delivered by computer. Usually used disparagingly because much early training on CBTs was little more than memory drills.

distance learning

> An earlier term for e-learning.

distributed learning

> An earlier term for e-learning.

e-learning

Education or training that uses technology. Commonly used to refer to training that is delivered over the Internet.

e-lectures

Another term for "Web lectures."

firewall

Software that lets only authorized persons into your company's internal communications network. For example, employees at home can dial in for e-mail and application access, but unauthorized users ("hackers") are rejected. Firewalls screen individual users and often have restrictions on the type and size of transmissions they will let through.

groupware

Industry term for software that lets teams of people collaborate.

instructor

A subject expert who is able to present the material so it gets across to the student. Traditionally found standing in front of a classroom. More and more found at a computer connected to the Internet.

instructor-led learning

A type of e-learning in which an instructor (or teacher) runs the course.

intellectual capital (IC)

Knowledge about how a company works at all levels, stored, categorized, and accessible electronically, much like in a library.

knowledge

The stuff you know about (compare to "skills"). It's the ability to tell what a roadsign means, in contrast to the ability to maneuver the car around a pothole.

knowledge management

An organized attempt at structuring the knowledge of an organization. Akin to the attempt of traditional librarians to organize the knowledge of culture and civilization, but done in a business for business purposes. (Not "knowledge for knowledge's sake.") Related to e-learning in much the same way that going to the public library to find books on mathematics is related to going to calculus class.

learning management system (LMS)

Software that provides the components needed to run an enterprisewide e-learning system. Includes such things as course catalog, course delivery mechanism, student registration, management reporting mechanism, and so on.

learning portal

A Web site designed to be the entry point for users to get to e-learning courses.

LMS

See "learning management system."

page turner

A type of Web-based training that mimics a book, where you proceed by "turning the pages" in a linear fashion. Sometimes called "Web books."

portal

See "learning portal."

real-time learning

See "synchronous learning."

scalability

The ability of a system to grow gracefully, without hitting artificial barriers. For example, scalable training will be able to handle a dozen, a hundred, or a thousand students with only minor additional investment in delivery resources. Nonscalable training on the other hand might be written to handle dozens of students and would need a complete rewrite to handle hundreds of students.

SCORM

An important industry standard for e-learning. It stands for "sharable content object reference model." See http://www.adlnet.org/Scorm/scorm.cfm.

self-directed learning

Learning that is directed by the student, without an instructor. Compare to "instructor-led learning."

self-paced learning

E-learning where the pace is controlled by the student. For example, students can choose to take a two-hour course in a single day, or in fifteen-minute chunks over several days. Commonly used as a synonym for self-directed learning.

skills

Things you can actually do, like play the piano, run a department, drive a car (compare to "knowledge").

synchronous learning

A type of learning in which the instructor and all the students are connected at the same time. Compare to "asynchronous learning."

team room

Another name for a Web page that acts as a bulletin board or discussion page for student–student or student–instructor communications.

threaded discussion

A discussion Web page that indicates which message postings are in reply to other messages so you can follow different discussion threads. Bill asks a question. Sue replies to Bill. Tom replies to Sue. Frank replies to Bill. Tom replies to Frank. Sue replies to Frank. Etc.

training management system (TMS)

A synonym for "learning management system."

virtual classroom

A phrase that implies achieving the classroom experience though your computer. Often implies an instructional design approach that mimics learning in a classroom.

WBT

See "Web-based training"

Web-based training (WBT)

Learning that is accessible from a Web page through a Web browser like Netscape Navigator. Usually implies training that is available at any time and at any place.

Web books

See "page turner."

Web lectures

Lectures that can be delivered over the Internet, usually as a recorded communication from the instructor to the students. Usually implies the transmission of audio and PowerPoint-type slides, and sometimes video.

Index